In God's Waiting Room

In God's Waiting Room

Learning Through Suffering

by
Lehman Strauss

MOODY PRESS
CHIGAGO

Library of Congress Cataloging in Publication Data

Strauss, Lehman.
 In God's waiting room.

 1. Strauss, Elsie—Health. 2. Cerebrovascular
disease—Patients—United States—Biography.
3. Consolation. 4. Christian life—1960-
I. Title.
RC388.5.S83S77 1985 248.8'6'0924 [B] 85-10674
ISBN 0-8024-3827-X (pbk.)

4 5 6 7 Printing/LC/Year 88 87

Printed in the United States of America

Contents

Preface

The first eight chapters of this book were written originally for Radio Bible Class and distributed to their large family of listeners and viewers via radio and television. They have graciously consented to allow Moody Press to reprint and publish the book.

I have since added the chapter "That Strange Love of God" and slightly revised several paragraphs. It is sent forth in the hope that a wider reading public will benefit from it.

Sickness can be one of life's most distressing and humbling circumstances, both for the person who is afflicted and for the loved ones who stand on the sidelines. This is particularly true of strokes, when both brain and body are affected. These two are intricately related, for the brain is the power station that controls the members of the body.

Having spent seventy-six consecutive days in the hospital watching the anguish and frustration of stroke victims, I have learned something of the depths of humiliation and helplessness to which we poor mortals can fall. This personal account is intended to give you understanding and help in responding to any troubling situation the Lord may allow to come into your life.

1

Great Moments in Marriage, and Then—

The year 1981 was a magnificent milestone for my wife Elsie and me. It was a year to which we looked forward and one we will never forget. That year marked our golden wedding anniversary. Fifty beautiful years!

Ours has not been a perfect marriage, of course. There cannot be a perfect marriage where two imperfect people are involved. But having listened to the complaints of hundreds of wives and husbands who have come to me for counsel, I do not hesitate to tell you that our marriage has been far above average. Sure, we have had problems, but we have learned how to resolve them.

Our marriage has been packed with great moments. We were married June 17, 1931. In preparation for that big event, I had spent just about every dollar I had saved. After the wedding, Elsie had sixty dollars; in fact, between the two of us we had sixty dollars! We enjoyed our honeymoon in Atlantic City—one week at the Blackstone Hotel. (In those days you got a lot for your money). What a week!

I wish I had the time and space to tell you about some of the wonderful moments we shared during our half-century together. But our 50th anniversary in 1981 was the best of all. Our families and friends had arranged celebrations, seven of them, from one end of our country to the other: in Escondido, California; Colorado Springs, Colorado; Detroit, Michigan; Middletown, North East, Maryland; Bristol, Pennsylvania; Schroon Lake, New York; and Charleston, West Virginia.

A full schedule of meetings had been planned through that summer and fall. It was without doubt the greatest year of our lives. After it was all over, we both relived with pleasure the joy of those glorious twelve months.

Meanwhile, we looked ahead to a full schedule of meetings in 1982. During January and February, I spoke forty-one times in Florida. Then we drove to our home in Escondido, California, for three weeks of rest and study. Our plans were for Elsie to remain home during the latter part of March and April while I journeyed east to resume my ministry.

Then it happened. On March 27, I arrived in Peoria, Illinois, to begin a one-week conference on prophecy under the direction of the Moody Bible Institute. I was sitting in the motel room beside the telephone on Sunday afternoon, waiting with joyful anticipation. It was prearranged that Elsie would call me at four o'clock, Illinois time. The telephone had been a vital link between us whenever I was away. A man many miles from the one he loves becomes lonely.

With the first ring of the telephone, I picked it up and answered. The voice I heard on the other end of the line, however, was not the one I expected. Our son Richard was calling.

"Dad, the news is not good. Mother had a stroke." He gave me what information he had. I told him I would make flight plans and call him back.

I put down the telephone and just sat there stunned. After fifty years of a happy and trial-free relationship, why should the roof cave in like this? That Sunday in March was the darkest day in all my seventy-one years. Now, as I write these lines, it is nine months to the day since Elsie was stricken. The severity of the trial has not diminished. At times it has been even more severe.

I have been teaching the Bible and preaching sermons and writing books for forty-five years. I have set forth fervently, and sometimes dogmatically, the great doctrines of our historical Christian faith. I sought to comfort, console, and cheer sorrowing and suffering Christians. But trial and tribulation are now my constant companions. Truths that I once knew intellectually and academically, I am now learning experientially. There is a great difference.

In this book I am writing the testimony of that which is taking place in my own life during these months of watching my dear Elsie suffer. Her stroke was serious, and her recovery limited. Since her discharge from the hospital in mid-June, I have been caring for her twenty-four hours every day. When you watch the one person suffer whom you love more than you love your own life, you reach a turning point. I am at that point now.

This is not the testimony of a hero who has been living victoriously on the mountaintop. Some days and nights I have been in the valley. Back in the 1940s the young people at the Pinebrook Summer Bible Conference in Pennsylvania used to sing the following chorus:

> Down in the dumps I'll never go,
> That's where the devil keeps me low,
> So I'll sing with all my might,
> And I'll keep my armor bright,
> But, down in the dumps I'll never go.
> (Author Unknown)

I sang that chorus many times those days, with good intentions. But I won't sing it now. From experience I know better. In recent months I have been in those "dumps" a few times. Thank God, I am not there now!

The Word of God has been my stronghold in these difficult days. One of the most significant statements of our Lord was spoken during His confrontation with Satan. He said, "Man shall not live by bread alone, but by every word that proceedeth out of the mouth of God" (Matthew 4:4). When Jesus spoke those words He was not minimizing the importance of food for the body. He was saying that man has needs other than physical and material, needs that call for complete dependence upon God. Paul wrote about the outward man and the inward man (2 Corinthians 4:16; see also Romans 7:22 and Ephesians 3:16). Both need to be fed, and each has its own prescribed diet.

In times of trial it is easy to give in to the weight of the problem. Sorrow, suffering, or loss has a way of draining us of the strength we need to bear up under the trial. That empty feeling within us cries for a means of finding peace. Some people turn to drink, expecting that the alcohol will meet their need. I have a friend who becomes a compulsive eater whenever he faces a serious problem. But what we put into the body, which is the outward man, can never feed the inner man, which Peter calls "the hidden man of the heart" (1 Peter 3:4). Our Lord said, "Man shall not live by bread alone, but by every word that proceedeth out of the mouth of God." When Satan tempted Him, He went immediately to the Holy Scriptures. Because He had not eaten food for forty days and nights, He was hungry and in need of physical nourishment. The devil, the author of false confidence, tempted our Lord to feed the body. Instead, Christ drew confidently from the Scriptures during His testing.

As I sat contemplating what my son had told me on the telephone about Elsie, my thoughts went immediately to this passage:

There hath no temptation taken you but such as is common to man: but God is faithful, who will not suffer you to be tempted above that ye are able; but will with the tempta-

tion also make a way to escape, that ye may be able to bear
it. (1 Corinthians 10:13)

I was reminded that nothing unique had happened to
Elsie and me. Our trial was a common one. I have learned
since then that in the United States more than 500,000
people each year have a stroke.

I received a similar reminder from these words of the
apostle Peter: "Beloved, think it not strange concerning
the fiery trial which is to try you, as though some strange
thing happened unto you" (1 Peter 4:12). Because we are
God's children, and because He permitted the trial, I knew
He would also provide for our every need. His fidelity and
faithfulness were my guarantee. This is not the mere fig-
ment of my imagination but the glorious fact that God
has been with me to keep me from being overwhelmed by
the trial. God is faithful.

A phone call to the airline ticket office informed me
that there were no flights leaving Peoria that Sunday
evening that would give me connections to Escondido. I
arranged a reservation on the earliest flight Monday morning, phoned Richard, and began to wait. I found myself in
God's waiting room.

Hospitals have waiting rooms—small enclosures where
people go to wait and hope for a favorable change in the
condition of a loved one. Many of the people I have seen in
hospital waiting rooms were anxious, worried, and frus-
trated.

I have been in God's waiting room since my wife had
her stroke. God in His faithfulness has enabled me to bear
the trial. Elsie remains paralyzed, and she needs my love
and care twenty-four hours every day. I too am waiting
and hoping for a favorable change; as I wait I am drawing
upon the infinite resources of God's grace. This unex-
pected trial has changed my well-laid plans, but I know
that God's plans are far better than mine.

Even so, this business of waiting is one tough assign-
ment. I had never learned experientially that waiting is a

necessary part of Christian training. This is my first experience in God's waiting room. If "Waiting 101" were an elective course in God's school, you may be certain I would not choose it. But God didn't give me a choice—it was a required course. He made the choice for me, knowing I needed it. So I continue to wait.

The Scriptures contain many exhortations for Christians to wait for the Lord to fulfill His plans in His time. David prayed. "Thou art the God of my salvation; on thee do I wait all the day" (Psalm 25:5). (I could add, *all the night*.) David learned to wait, and he found it to be a profitable experience. He wrote, "Wait on the Lord: be of good courage, and He shall strengthen thine heart: wait, I say, on the Lord" (Psalm 27:14).

At times I have found it hard to wait. I get in a hurry, and God seems so slow. But I am learning that "they that wait upon the Lord shall renew their strength; they shall mount up with wings as eagles; they shall run, and not be weary; and they shall walk, and not faint" (Isaiah 40:31). This verse, as well as others like it, is proving to be blessedly true as I remain in God's waiting room.

I have always had the ambition and desire to do God's work. Since leaving the pastorate in 1963, I have averaged about 60,000 miles of travel annually, spoken 400 messages each year before audiences, and taught the Bible twenty-five minutes each weekday on the national radio program "Bible Study Time." It has been difficult to say no when invitations come to teach and preach God's Word. For the present, I do not have a choice. On April 1, 1982, I canceled all scheduled meetings for the twelve months following. I am thankful for more time to wait before the Lord in prayer. I am also grateful for the privilege of ministering to my dear Elsie.

Recently I read again the Twenty-third Psalm. Verse 2 came alive to me with fresh insight: "He maketh me to lie down in green pastures." He *maketh* me. I had always been active in Christian service, but I now have the feeling that I was busier than God wanted me to be. So I asked myself, "Is it possible that because God loves me, He allowed this painful trial to make me lie down?" Think about it.

I see a close connection between Psalm 23:2 and Mark 6:31, where our Lord said to His disciples: "Come ye yourselves apart into a desert place, and rest a while: for there were many coming and going, and they had no leisure so much as to eat." This statement of our Lord immediately followed the disciples' return from their first preaching mission. I detect in Mark 6:30 a bit of pride as the disciples reported to Christ all they had accomplished.

Note the point of likeness between Psalm 23:2 and Mark 6:31. The psalmist said, "He maketh me to lie down in green pastures." Mark records that the disciples were too busy to eat. We know Mark was speaking of food for the body, but we may profit from a spiritual application as well. We need to get alone with God and allow the Good Shepherd to lead us to fresh pastures of the Scriptures. If we will not do so voluntarily, then He will make us lie down.

One of my regrets is that I didn't take more time to lie down in the green pastures of God's Word during those busy years. I did read and study my Bible daily, but much of that reading and studying was to keep up with the demands of my speaking schedule.

Today I am grateful that God has made me lie down in the fresh green pastures of His Word. During these months of trial He has enabled me to experience the preciousness and power of His truth. My Good Shepherd has fed my soul, and I have not lacked one thing that is necessary and good. The green pastures of the Shepherd's Word are a sharp contrast to the dry desert wastelands of this world.

Nothing is wrong with sincere ambition and the desire to keep busy in God's work, but we need resting places along the way. God said to Elijah, "Hide thyself" (1 Kings 17:3), and then He appeared to Elijah saying, "Go, shew thyself" (1 Kings 18:1). The prophet needed time alone

with God before he could face the wicked Ahab. We all
must learn sooner or later that we too need time alone
with the Good Shepherd.

The flight home from Peoria on March 29 was a new
experience for me. I have flown more than a million miles
in the past fifty years, but this trip was different. At times
it seemed that this flight alone was a million miles. There
I was, a lonely man sitting in a plane, yet surrounded by
people. I did not know the seriousness of Elsie's illness. I
only knew that she had a stroke. I couldn't think of anything or anyone except Elsie. I felt bleak and desolate.
Never had I known such loneliness. I breathed a weak
prayer, "Dear Lord, help me!" I wanted to say more, but I
just couldn't articulate. I can't remember when I felt so
drained, so utterly weak—too weak to pray.

But God came to me in a most comforting and consol-
ing way by calling to my mind one of His precious promises. I had memorized it as a young Christian. "My presence
shall go with thee, and I will give thee rest" (Exodus
33:14). I am aware of the fact that some scholars punctu-
ate this verse as a question, and they could be correct. But
in my mind, there was no question about God's presence
being with me on my flight home. The Holy Spirit ministered assurance and peace as He brought other portions of
Scripture to my remembrance. "When thou passest through
the waters, I will be with thee" (Isaiah 43:2). "And the
LORD, he it is that doth go before thee" (Deuteronomy
31:8). "Fear thou not; for I am with thee" (Isaiah 41:10). I
did not need to ask God to be with me, for He has promised to be with me. He kept His promise!

One of the blessings of this trial came to me as I was
led from the "He" to the "thou" of Psalm 23—"*He* maketh
me to lie down. . . . *thou* art with me" (italics added).
There is a difference between talking about the Lord and
speaking directly to Him. In the latter, the waiting room
becomes the presence room. The Good Shepherd's presence continues to comfort and strengthen me. There were
days and nights when, looking through these human eyes,

I couldn't see any light at the end of the tunnel. But in those darkest moments Christ's presence provided comfort and care.

I am writing these lines on a dull, drab day. Stroke patients can be up one day and down the next. Today is a down day for Elsie. The burden has not lightened, and I have no idea what the outcome will be. But one thing is certain—my heart has found a resting place.

Our Lord said, "I will never leave thee [not ever, at any time], nor forsake thee" (Hebrews 13:5). That is His *promise!* The same verse contains a *precept,* "Be content with such things as ye have." I do not know if the Lord will heal Elsie, but I do know that He will never leave us nor forsake us.

The devil has tried to dissuade me, to turn me from Christ, to stir up a spirit of discontent within me. But he has not succeeded! The presence of Christ has made me satisfied with my state. The Christian standard of contentment is a lofty one. It would be beyond my reach, if it were not for the presence of my Lord. I have what the world cannot give. I have Christ. No one can improve on that!

I cannot say with the apostle Paul that "I have learned, in whatsoever state I am, therewith to be content" (Philippians 4:11). But I can testify that I am learning "through Christ which strengtheneth me" (Philippians 4:13).

The flight from Peoria to California was a lonely one, but I was not alone. I say to my suffering brothers and sisters in Christ—rest assured that our Lord will never desert you.

God is the creator and controller of the universe and all that is in it, whether animate or inanimate. Any use or disposition He chooses to make of any part of His creation is His sovereign right.

God is accountable only to Himself. He reports to nobody. He is not required at any time to give to any person any explanation for anything He says or does. He is the superpower above all powers in every area of His creation.

We do not expect to understand fully the purpose for our trials until our Lord calls us home to be with Him. But we do know that He loves us too much to harm us, and that He is far more concerned with our welfare than we are.

God's choices are always right. He is capable of carrying out any project to a successful conclusion without the possibility of fault or failure. Nothing in His universe happens by chance or accident. For every effect there is a cause. God "worketh all things after the counsel of His own will: That we should be to the praise of his glory" (Ephesians 1:11-12). Yes, God is in control.

2

God Is in Control

It was Wednesday, April 14, 1982. Eighteen days had passed since Elsie's stroke. The neurologist in charge requested that I meet with him. I waited expectantly in the corridor outside Elsie's room. When the doctor appeared his remarks were brief and pointed.

"We are making arrangements to move your wife to a rehabilitation center in San Diego."

"What led you to this decision?" I asked.

He hesitated. I detected a bit of concern in his delayed reply. I was right. His words came slowly.

"There is nothing more that we can do medically for Mrs. Strauss." He placed his hand on my shoulder and patted it gently. "I'm sorry," he said, and he walked away.

For a few seconds I stood motionless, my mind almost blank. Then I walked slowly into the room, kissed Elsie, and sat in the chair beside the bed.

She spoke first. "What did the doctor tell you?"

"He said that you will be transferred to a rehabilitation center in San Diego."

I took her hand in mine. Then I assured her that there was nothing to fear because God was in control.

But did I really believe that God was in control? The mere thought of questioning the sovereignty of God scared me. But then, the government of the universe is a question with which most of us have grappled at some time. We Christians affirm our belief in the sovereignty of God, but our faith is challenged in times of natural upheaval, national disaster, or personal affliction. Pain and poverty, disease and death, sorrow and suffering all tend to cause us to think seriously about God as creator and controller of the world of which we are a part. It is not always easy to believe that God is in control.

On that Wednesday in April 1982, my faith was being tested. At that particular moment my mind was not capable of rationalizing the majesty of God's sovereignty. When I was told the seriousness of Elsie's condition, I realized that some cherished plans would have to be canceled. Quite frankly, I could not understand God's reason for this turn of events. But I knew that the Bible contains all we poor mortals need to know. Our Lord said, "It is written, Man shall not live by bread alone, but by every word that proceedeth out of the mouth of God" (Matthew 4:4). So I went immediately to the Scriptures for help.

God's Sovereignty and the Scriptures

Although the words *sovereign* and *sovereignty* do not appear in the King James Version of the Bible, the fact of God's sovereignty is its major message.

The word *sovereign* comes from the Latin word *super*. It conveys the idea of superior and supreme, primary and paramount, unequaled and unexcelled. The God of the Bible is eternal and self-existent. He is supreme in excellence and perfect in all His ways. He is the one and only autonomist, self-contained and self-controlled, with the right and power of self-government. God is infinite in His imperial independence. His capacities and capabilities far surpass the scope of human reasons.

After Elsie had her stroke, someone sent her a book entitled *Yet Will I Trust Him* by Peg Rankin. The book is nontechnical and nontheological, but we found it to be practical and helpful. It contains this brief definition of God's sovereignty, "God can do anything He wants to do, anytime He wants to do it, anyway He wants to do it, and for any purpose He wants to accomplish." Any use or disposition God chooses to make of any part of His creation, animate or inanimate, is His sovereign right. When God revealed to Abraham that He would destroy Sodom and Gomorrah, the patriarch knew that many people would die. To that frightening revelation Abraham said, "Shall not the Judge of all the earth do right?" (Genesis 18:25).

In addition to being sovereign, God is righteous. This means that He can do no wrong. If God could do wrong, He would cease to be God. When those two cities were destroyed, God was in control. He was doing what He wanted to do, when He wanted to do it, in the way He wanted to do it, and for the purpose He wanted to accomplish. And in so doing, He did right.

The book of Daniel was written to teach the sovereign rule of God over all nations on earth. Read these excerpts:

> —to the intent that the living may know that the most High ruleth in the kingdom of men, and giveth it to whomsoever he will, and setteth up over it the basest of men. (4:17)

> —till thou know that the most High ruleth in the kingdom of men, and giveth it to whomsoever he will. (4:25)

> —until thou know that the most High ruleth in the kingdom of men, and giveth it to whomsoever he will. (4:32)

> And [Nebuchadnezzar] was driven from the sons of men; and his heart was made like the beasts, and his dwelling was with the wild asses; they fed him with grass like oxen, and his body was wet with the dew of heaven; till he

knew that the most high God ruled in the kingdom of men,
and that he appointeth over it whomsoever He will. (5:21)

In each of the above passages the name "most High" or
"most high God" is used. It is the Hebrew name *El Elyon*,
and means "the possessor of heaven and earth" (Genesis
14:22). The Holy Spirit guided the writers of Scripture to
state emphatically that "the earth is the Lord's, and the
fulness thereof; the world, and they that dwell therein"
(Psalm 24:1; see also 1 Corinthians 10:26, 28). God sent
the plagues upon the Egyptians so that the people would
know "that the earth is the Lord's" (Exodus 9:29). The
universe is God's by creative right. By Him were all things
created and by Him all things consist (see Colossians
1:16-17; Hebrews 1:3).

The apostle declared that God "worketh all things
after the counsel of his own will" (Ephesians 1:11). Civili-
zations have risen and fallen. Great leaders of nations
have reigned and have been dethroned. And all the while,
God has been in control. David prayed to the Lord, "Both
riches and honour come of thee, and thou reignest over
all" (1 Chronicles 29:12). With the rise and fall of every
world ruler, God has been in control. Yes, He has been
doing what He wanted to do, when He wanted to do it, in
the way He wanted to do it, for the purpose He wanted to
accomplish, and using whomever He would.

Likewise, the book of Amos teaches the sovereign control of God over all the affairs in heaven and on earth. The
nation of Israel had willfully disobeyed God. Divine judg-
ment came to the people in several ways: war, drought,
famine, and plagues of grasshoppers. Read chapter 4 carefully and note the seven times God said to Israel that He
was responsible for every disaster that befell the nation.
Observe the use of the first person singular: "I also have
given you ... want of bread" (v. 6); "I have withholden
the rain from you" (v. 7); "I have smitten you with blast-
ing and mildew" (v. 9); "I have sent among you the pesti-
lence after the manner of Egypt" (v. 10); "I have overthrown

some of you" (v. 11). God here informed the nation that He was the motivating force behind disease, death, drought, and destruction.

Now look at Amos 3:6, where the prophet asked, "Shall there be evil in a city, and the Lord hath not done it?" The word *evil* here does not refer to moral evil, but rather a calamity. Through the prophet Isaiah, God said, "I form the light, and create darkness: I make peace, and create evil: I, the Lord, do all these things" (45:7). Again the word *evil* denotes any kind of a natural disaster such as a plague, drought, flood, or earthquake.

Both Amos and Isaiah are telling us that nothing happens by chance or accident. For every effect there is a cause. God does what He wants to do, when He wants to do it, in the way He wants to do it, for the purpose He wants to accomplish, and involves any person or persons He chooses to use.

The supreme rulership of God is based upon the perfections of His divine being. This is the biblical concept of God, and Christians need to believe it and hold fast to it. God is the supreme dispenser of all events. "He ruleth by His power for ever" (Psalm 66:7). He is "the blessed and only Potentate, the King of kings, and Lord of lords" (1 Timothy 6:15). Our loving Heavenly Father is the sovereign ruler over all His creation. He is in control. This is the plain teaching of the Holy Scriptures.

God's Sovereignty and Human Suffering

I am learning that there is a large gap between studying truth intellectually and knowing that truth by personal experience. This fact was made real to me as I reviewed what the Bible teaches about the sovereignty of God. Quite frankly, I confess to having had a bit of a problem on the day of April 14, 1982.

This was my problem: How does a child of God reconcile God's sovereignty with human suffering and affliction? How does a Christian apply the sovereignty of God when his wife, whom he loves more than he loves his own life, lies helpless and suffering before him?

If someone had come to me on that day in April and said, "I would like to help you. What are your needs?" I wouldn't have had any answer. My mind was too boggled. I was hurting. I needed time for in-depth study and personal application of the truth of God's sovereignty.

Is it wrong for a minister and teacher of God's Word to be perplexed? Although most of us don't admit it, all of us at some time have been tempted to walk away from God. But when a hurting person takes his view of life from what he is experiencing, from what he sees and feels, that's one time when he needs to draw near to God. As the apostle James put it, "Draw nigh to God, and he will draw nigh to you" (James 4:8). Asaph was perplexed by what he saw in life, but he came to the right conclusion when he said, "But it is good for me to draw near to God" (Psalm 73:28).

How do I draw near to God? I could pray. But at that moment I was affected emotionally to the point where I couldn't articulate an intelligent prayer. Then too, what could I tell God that He didn't already know? I needed to draw near to God, not to update Him on Elsie's condition and our needs. I needed to draw near so that He could speak to me and give me the assurance that He was in control. I had just told Elsie that God was in control. But at that moment, I was being controlled by an experience that perplexed me. So I drew near to God through His Word.

The prophet Isaiah wrote, "And though the Lord give you the bread of adversity, and the water of affliction—" (Isaiah 30:20). Yes, God does send adversity and affliction to His own. They are His gifts to us, "For whom the Lord loveth he chasteneth" (Hebrews 12:6). This is a time of adversity and affliction for Elsie and me, but I will not dishonor the Lord by questioning His right to do what He wants to do.

I see no difference between a God who is not sovereign and no God at all. If I were to doubt now that the Lord of the Bible, the God and Father of every believer in the Lord Jesus Christ, is in control over our lives, I would be no better than an atheist.

David stood before the congregation and prayed aloud to God, "Thine, O Lord, is the greatness, and the power, and the glory, and the victory, and the majesty: for all that is in the heaven and in the earth is thine; thine is the kingdom, O Lord, and thou art exalted as head above all. Both riches and honour come of thee, and thou reignest over all" (1 Chronicles 29:11-12). Take special note of that word *reignest*. Because it is in the present continuous tense, it tells us that God is reigning now. At this very moment God is in control.

I am comforted with the assurance that my Lord has a good and wise purpose to be served through Elsie's affliction. Exactly what His purpose is in sending this trial into our lives I do not know at this time. Nor do I know if God will ever reveal His purpose to us in this life. The Lord said, "What I do thou knowest not now; but thou shalt know hereafter" (John 13:7). I do not want these words of our Lord to be lost on me as they were lost on Peter. One day Elsie and I will understand that which for the present is hidden from us. We can afford to wait. "For now we see through a glass, darkly; but then, face to face: now I know in part; but then shall I know even as also I am known" (1 Corinthians 13:12).

Multitudes have suffered and died, and multitudes continue to suffer, without knowing the reason why. The Bible says, "There hath no temptation taken you but such as is common to man: but God is faithful, who will not suffer you to be tempted above that ye are able; but will with the temptation also make a way to escape, that ye may be able to bear it" (1 Corinthians 10:13). This is God's promise that He will place a limit upon the severity of the trial and that He will give us sufficient strength to bear up under it.

We realize that we are not the only ones to suffer

without knowing the reason. Job, for instance, who suffered great losses and bore heavy burdens, never did learn
the reason the tragedies came into his life.

Recently, as I reread Psalm 119, I was greatly im-
pressed and encouraged with David's personal testimony
of the blessings he received from the afflictions he suffered.

First, *he bore witness to the sovereignty of God* when he
was afflicted. He said, "I know, O Lord, that thy judg-
ments are right, and that thou in faithfulness has afflicted
me" (v. 75). Here we have a clear testimony, given by
divine inspiration, that God in righteousness sent affliction into David's life and experience.

Second, David testified that *affliction was a learning
experience for him*. He wrote, "It is good for me that I have
been afflicted; that I might learn thy statutes" (v. 71).
Suffering is a required course in God's school, and it
should be a great learning place for every believer in the
Lord Jesus Christ. Our trial has been for me an enriching
experience. It has taught me some valuable lessons.

Third, David testified how *his affliction benefited him
spiritually*. "Before I was afflicted I went astray: but now
have I kept thy word" (v. 67). One of the proverbs reminds
us that "whom the Lord loveth He correcteth; even as a
father the son in whom he delighteth" (Proverbs 3:12).
The New Testament adds witness to this fact with the
words, "For whom the Lord loveth He chasteneth, and
scourgeth every son whom He receiveth" (Hebrews 12:6).

Yes, spiritual benefits are to be derived from trials
and suffering. God has placed us on earth that we may
glorify Him. "Yet if any man suffer as a Christian, let him
not be ashamed; but let him glorify God on this behalf" (1
Peter 4:16). The suffering season of life is a beautiful time
to glorify God. It provides us with a fresh incentive to
grow in grace and to develop spiritually.

Every afflicted Christian should bow to the absolute
sovereignty of God and surrender to Him the right to do
what He chooses to do, whenever He chooses to do it, in

any way He chooses to do it, for any purpose He wants to accomplish, and to use any person He chooses.

He Maketh No Mistake

My Father's way may twist and turn,
   My heart may throb and ache,
But in my soul I'm glad I know
   He maketh no mistake.

My cherished plans may go astray,
   My hopes may fade away,
But still I'll trust my Lord to lead,
   For He doth know the way.

Though night be dark and it may seem
   That day will never break,
I'll pin my faith, my all in Him,
   He maketh no mistake.

There's so much now I cannot see,
   My eyesight's far too dim;
But come what may, I'll surely trust
   And leave it all to Him.

For by and by the mist will lift
   And plain it all He'll make;
Through all the way, though dark to me,
   He made not one mistake.
                              (A.M. Overton)

The child of God must be continually mindful that his Heavenly Father programs everything that happens to him. The trials that come, whether slight or severe, are for his good. An understanding of this truth will give the believer in Christ the assurance of safety and security.

There is great peace in the knowledge of the father-child relationship the Christian has with God. Whether or not things are going well, it is possible for every believer in Christ to say with Job, "Though he slay me, yet will I trust in him" (Job 13:15).

3

The Arrows
of the Almighty

If ever a man was justified in asking why he was afflicted with sorrow and suffering, Job was that man. He needed all the help he could get. What he did not need was someone to add to his burden and aggravate his problem.

Eliphaz, one of Job's friends, believed that the sickness and suffering he was experiencing could be explained only on the basis of some sin in his life. He sought to impress upon Job his philosophy that righteous people are not made to suffer; therefore, Job's trial was the result of his own wrongdoing (Job 4:7-8). But Eliphaz was wrong! The accusations he leveled against Job only added to the patriarch's misery.

Bad things do happen to good people, even to the best of the good ones. Job was one of the choicest among God's people. The Lord Himself testified of Job that there was none like him in the earth, that he was a perfect and an upright man, and that he feared God and hated evil (Job 1:1, 8).

Job was known for being *faithful*. He was not sinless, as the word *perfect* in verses 1 and 8 might imply. A better word might be *blameless*, meaning that he was ethically upright, morally above reproach, and religiously devoted to God. Job had a deep and devout reverence for the Lord. His consistent practice was to hold God in highest awe and respect. He was faithful.

Job was known for his *fortune*. "His substance also was seven thousand sheep, and three thousand camels, and five hundred yoke of oxen, and five hundred she asses, and a very great household" (Job 1:3). He possessed vast wealth, and it was God who had caused him to prosper (Job 1:10, 21).

Job was known for his *family*. "And there were born unto him seven sons and three daughters" (Job 1:2). Job's family and his fortune were the blessings of God. The record shows that Job loved his family. His love for God was reflected in his love for his children. As the spiritual leader of his family, he carried them all in his prayers to God. The highest service a parent can render to his children is to care for their spiritual welfare. Job was a good family man.

Finally, Job was a man of *fame*. The inspired record says he was "the greatest of all the men of the east" (Job 1:3). Job stood head and shoulders above the men of his day. He rated high with both man and God. God Himself affirmed that He had no reason to afflict Job (Job 2:3).

Yet God allowed Job to go through a deep valley and subjected him to a severe trial. Most of us would have cracked under the same conditions. How are we to understand the sorrows and sufferings of Job? How can we enter into the meaning of his adversities and afflictions?

The first two chapters of this ancient book contain the essentials to understanding its message. During World War II, I was serving God in a pastorate in Bristol, Pennsylvania. Then news came that one of the charter members of that church had been killed in action while serving his country. I prepared a message that I hoped would be appropriate for the occasion, one that would meet some of the needs of that soldier's hurting parents. I entitled the sermon, "Why Righteous People Suffer." I still have the pulpit notes I made of that sermon. In my introduction I said that the book of Job was written to tell us why God's children suffer.

Forty years have passed since I preached that sermon. I would not preach it today as I preached it then. That is because the message of the book of Job is not "why God's children are caused to suffer," but rather "the sovereignty of God." It tells us that God is always in control in every situation at all times. Nothing happens to us by chance or accident. For every effect there is a cause. If we fail to see this great truth in the book of Job, we have missed its major message.

The First Affliction

Act One in this drama presents a scene in heaven. The angelic creatures, fallen and unfallen, are made to appear before the Lord. God remains in control, demanding that angels and demons report to Him. Among them stands Satan, whose name means "the adversary." He is no ordinary human adversary; rather, he is a superhuman spirit being, the one who beguiled Eve through his subtlety (2 Corinthians 11:3). He has continued to harass God's children ever since. The apostle Peter warned believers, "Be sober, be vigilant; because your adversary the devil, as a roaring lion walketh about, seeking whom he may devour" (1 Peter 5:8). Job was one of Satan's targets.

It all began with a conversation in heaven between God and Satan.

> And the Lord said unto Satan, Hast thou considered my servant Job, that there is none like him in the earth, a perfect and an upright man, one that feareth God, and escheweth evil?
>
> Then Satan answered the Lord, and said, Doth Job fear God for naught?

Hast not thou made an hedge about him, and about his
house, and about all that he hath on every side? thou hast
blessed the work of his hands, and his substance is in-
creased in the land.

But put forth thine hand now, and touch all that he
hath, and he will curse thee to thy face. (Job 1:8-11)

Here Satan accused Job of serving God because of the
blessings God bestowed upon him. In substance, the devil
told God that Job served Him, not because he loved and
revered Him but because of what he had received from
God. Satan then challenged God to put Job to the test by
taking his possessions from him. This was Satan's accusation against Job: Those who profess to love God and worship Him do so only because God provides for them
materially and protects them.

But something was involved in Satan's charge that
goes much deeper than his accusation against Job. He was
attacking the character of God. In essence, Satan said,
"You tell me that Job loves and serves You out of respect
and reverence for You. Let me tell you the real reason he
worships You. You bribed him. You bought him for a
price. Men and women do not worship You from a heart
of love. They do it for what they get out of it. Everything
man does in obedience to You, he does for personal gain.
You know this is true, so You give him the good things of
life to win his love and devotion."

In this sneering charge, Satan did not merely impugn
Job's motive for serving God, but he slandered God's motive for giving possessions and protection to Job. He was
actually slandering the character of God. Satan argued
that if God were to take Job's possessions from him the
patriarch would cease to be loyal to Him.

A conflict grew out of that conversation in heaven
between God and Satan. God's character had been challenged, and the adversary had to be proven wrong. So,
permission was given to Satan to put Job to the test. God
gave Satan the liberty to take away Job's possessions.

This liberty was limited, however, to all that was involved in the hedge to which Satan referred in Job 1:10. Satan was restrained from touching his person (Job 1:12). The sovereignty of God is seen in the limitations that He placed upon Satan. The test would prove Satan wrong. He must learn that Job was not serving God for personal gain.

Satan proceeded to the outer limits of those restrictions. In a swift succession of events, Job's possessions, which had taken him almost a lifetime to accumulate, were stripped from him. Thieving bands of Sabeans and Chaldeans raided the livestock and killed the hired hands. Lightning bolts destroyed the 7,000 sheep and the shepherds. The climax of the disaster came when a tornado destroyed the house, killing all of Job's children (Job 1:13-19). Job was put to the ultimate test. He was crushed by the report of the losses. This was Job's severest trial, his deepest valley.

Keep in mind that Job did not have the faintest idea of why it had all happened. He did not know that God had chosen him as His special instrument to demonstrate that men do love and serve Him because He is God, and to defend the character of God. To Job, the trial was without meaning and understanding. But as we shall see, Job did prove that a man's love and devotion to God can be genuine, even in the bitterest of trials.

> Then Job arose, and rent his mantle, and shaved his head, and fell down upon the ground, and worshipped.
> And said, Naked came I out of my mother's womb, and naked shall I return thither: the Lord gave, and the Lord hath taken away; blessed be the name of the Lord. (Job 1:20-21).

Rending his robe and shaving his head were signs of grief. These were rites of mourning. Falling to the ground was not an act of desperation, but a deed of reverence and submission before God. In so doing, Job "worshipped" (1:20).

G. Campbell Morgan in *The Analyzed Bible* said, "Job

is powerless against his enemy up to a certain point. There is, however, an inner citadel which the enemy cannot touch." Peter called it "the hidden man of the heart" (1 Peter 3:4). And Paul said, "though our outward man perish, yet the inward man is renewed day by day" (2 Corinthians 4:16). The "outward man" of which Paul spoke corresponds to the "earthen vessels" (4:7), "the body" (4:10), and "our mortal flesh" (4:11). The body is our physical, mortal frame, and it is decaying. Everything—our frame, faculties, family, fame, and fortune—is steadily decaying through an irreversible process. As the things of this earth fade, the things of the Spirit, which are eternal, become more precious.

Job's losses no doubt taxed his physical strength, but Satan could not reach his inner nature. Satan cannot touch the life that his hidden with Christ in God (Colossians 3:3). Job learned that "a man's life consisteth not in the abundance of the things which he possesseth" (Luke 12:15). There was a light in his soul that Satan could not extinguish. Job proved that a child of God will love and serve Him even though all material things are taken from him.

Perhaps the greatest testimony of Job's faith is in his words following Satan's first assault upon him. He said, "Naked came I out of my mother's womb, and naked shall I return thither: the Lord gave, and the Lord hath taken away; blessed be the name of the Lord" (Job 1:21). Ponder those words seriously and soberly. They witness to Job's faith in the sovereignty of God—the fact that God is in full control of His universe, including the earth and all created things in it, animate and inanimate. Any disposition God chooses to make of any part of His creation is His sovereign right. God gave Job his family and his fortune, and God took them from him. Job's faith in God was victoriously vindicated, as was God's faith in Job. Job did not curse God as Satan predicted (1:11); rather, he praised God (1:21).

Job's personal relationship with God remained at the highest level, in spite of the bitter experiences that had touched his life. His trial only deepened his faith and drew him closer to God. He praised the Lord when his family and fortune were given to him, and he continued to praise Him when the Lord took them from him.

Christians should never question the sovereignty of God. Our Heavenly Father never makes a mistake. When we believe this, we prove the devil to be wrong in his estimate of God and His children.

The Second Affliction

Chapter 2 in the book of Job records the second trial Job suffered. The second council meeting in heaven followed the pattern of the first. Once more the angels appeared before God, and Satan again presented himself. The Lord once more spoke His thoughts about His servant Job (Job 2:1-3). But this time He added the words, "And still he holdeth fast his integrity, although thou movedst me against him, to destroy him without cause" (Job 2:3).

God restated His faith in Job's integrity and reminded Satan that his accusation against Job was without foundation ("without cause"). Satan's lie about Job was disproved.

Satan accused God again of protecting Job, insisting that the restrictions God had placed upon him were a hindrance in proving his charge against Job. He could not deny that the loss of Job's family and his fortune had not lessened his loyalty to God. Even so, Satan made no mention of Job's faithfulness to God or to his own failure.

> And Satan answered the Lord, and said, Skin for skin, yea, all that a man hath will he give for his life.
> But put forth thine hand now, and touch his bone and his flesh, and he will curse thee to thy face. (Job 2:4-5)

Satan was saying that a man is not really tested until his own flesh and bones are made to suffer. Any person will surrender his possessions as long as he himself is spared.

The word *life* in verse 4 has reference to Job's person, his body. H. H. Rowley comments, "Job's life is not in question here, since if he were killed the motive of his piety could not thereby be determined." Satan was asking God for permission to afflict Job's body. Death would be easier than painful, agonizing suffering; so, if Job were subjected to torture, he would renounce God. Satan's language clearly shows his low estimate of a true child of God.

"And the Lord said unto Satan, Behold, he is in thine hand; but save his life" (Job 2:6). God accepted Satan's challenge but gave this limitation: Satan could not kill him. The word *life* in verse 6 is rendered differently from that in verse 4.

So the devil went forth with a vicious vengeance to do his ugly work against the good man of God. "Satan . . . smote Job with sore boils from the sole of his foot unto his crown" (Job 2:7). Let us not lose sight of the fact that the physical affliction of Job was added to a sorrow that was already deep in his heart, the grief over the death of his children and the loss of his earthly possessions.

Has ever a man or a woman, apart from our Lord Jesus Christ, been in a valley so deep or suffered a trial so severe? I think not. Burning ulcers like a leprosy covered Job's body, causing him great pain and agony. The symptoms mentioned in the book of Job are many: inflamed eruptions (2:7); maggots in the ulcers (7:5); terrifying dreams (7:14); running tears blinding the eyes (16:16); fetid breath (19:17); emaciated body (19:20); erosion of the bones (30:17); blackening and peeling off of the skin (30:30). Satan went to the limit to turn Job against God.

Adding to Job's anguish of body and mind was the reaction of his wife. She said to him, "Dost thou still retain thine integrity? curse God, and die" (Job 2:9). Frankly, I do not know what prompted her to speak as she did. I suspect that she did not know God intimately and personally as Job did, for she blamed God for the adversity and affliction that had come into their home. Her attitude seems to have been a reflection of her mental and spiritual condition. After all, she suffered the same losses as Job did. But now she could only stand by helplessly and watch him suffer. It was more than she could endure. Whatever prompted her to suggest that he renounce God and die could only add to Job's suffering.

His answer to his wife, his one remaining treasure on earth, in no way casts doubt upon his love for her. It does declare, however, his unswerving love and loyalty to God. By using a simple question, he testified to the sovereignty of God in everything that touched their lives, both good and bad: "What? Shall we receive good at the hand of God, and shall we not receive evil?" (Job 2:10). With this question, Job sought to help her see that she should be as willing as he was to accept the bitter as well as the better. It is a reminder of the sovereign right of God to do what He wants to do, when He decides to do it, for the purpose He chooses to accomplish, and to involve whomever He will. The person who truly loves God is willing to accept from His hand not only the good things but also affliction and adversity.

We are told that "in all this did not Job sin with his lips" (Job 2:10). He passed the test with a perfect grade. Satan had been defeated. Moreover, the devil does not appear again in the entire book of Job.

As I studied these two chapters in Job, the question God asked twice of Satan challenged me. It was as though the Lord asked me, "Have you considered My servant Job?" Have I learned the lesson of Job's experience? Is my will totally surrendered to God's will, as was Job's? Do I love my Lord and bow before Him in worship now that Elsie remains paralyzed and suffers? Can I say sincerely from a dedicated heart, "The Lord gave, and the Lord hath taken away; blessed be the name of the Lord"?

I am thankful for what God has taught me as I remain in His waiting room. I feel as David felt during his time of trial, when he prayed, "It is good for me that I have been afflicted; that I might learn thy statutes" (Psalm 119:71).

The waiting room has truly been my learning place. And
if I have learned nothing else from this experience, I now
know that I had much to learn.

I expect to meet Job one day. I will thank him for the
rich legacy. He has helped me to regard my trial, not as
the fiery darts of Satan (Ephesians 6:16) but as "the arrows of the Almighty" (Job 6:4). He who sent the arrows
has bound up and dressed the wounds. In His own time,
and for His good purpose, He will heal them perfectly.
"Though he slay me, yet will I trust in him" (Job 13:15).

Sometimes in the vale of suffering we are emotionally, physically, and spiritually down. We are in desperate need, feeling that we are unable to go on. It is then, more than ever, that we need to claim God's promise to assist us.

At one of those down times with Elsie, I realized with new clarity the truth of Hebrews 4:16: "Let us therefore come boldly unto the throne of grace, that we may obtain mercy, and find grace to help in time of need."

In the precious words of this passage, we are told of a place to go in time of need, a procedure to follow, the purpose for going, and the Person to whom we flee. This verse tells us what to do when we feel we're about to be overwhelmed, and it holds a tremendous promise.

Our sovereign Lord does not leave us to ourselves in a time of suffering. He does not leave us with no course of action, no place to turn. The invitation of Hebrews 4:16 is open to all who are in God's waiting room. If you are there, I urge you to accept it as I did one lonely night.

4

In Time of Need

May 14, 1982, was not a good day for Elsie. Both physically and emotionally she was having one of those down days. I arrived home from the hospital about 8:30 that night, physically weary and emotionally drained. Watching her suffer and struggle for the past ten hours had gotten to me.

I sat in my favorite chair and slumped into a spell of self-pity, dwelling on my own sorrow. The tears flowed freely. The longer I sat there feeling sorry for myself, the more depressed I became. I felt myself slipping into a state of despondency. There was no drive or desire to do anything.

Very early that same morning, I had typed Hebrews 4:16 on a file card and taken it with me to the hospital. During the day I had read it to Elsie several times, and together we had come several times to God's throne of grace.

Now I was the one who had the need. The time had arrived for me to translate our verse into my own experi-

ence. The content of this chapter is the message God gave
to me on the night of May 14, 1982.

"Let us, therefore, come boldly unto the throne of
grace, that we may obtain mercy, and find grace to help
in time of need" (Hebrews 4:16). Is today a time of need
for you? Here is a text which promises some very special
help. Many of God's children have put it to the test and
found that it works.

A Place

This verse tells us first of all that we have a *place* we
can go in time of need. That place is God's throne of
grace. This throne is unusual and different in that judg-
ment does not issue from it. At a future time there will
appear "a great white throne" from which God will judge
all who have rejected His Son, the Lord Jesus Christ. But
none of God's children will appear before that throne, for
all who stand before Him in that day will be "cast into
the lake of fire" (Revelation 20:11-15). During the present
dispensation of grace, however, God's throne is "the throne
of grace."

Beloved Christian, are you acquainted with this place?
When did you last appear before the throne of grace? Our
text says, "Let us come." I have been to that place many
times, sometimes on my knees, at other times when lying
in bed, driving my automobile, walking, or traveling in a
plane or train. I am thankful that I have a place where I
can go in time of need.

I have just come from that blessed throne. The burden has been lifted. Right now there is a fresh awareness
of God's grace and mercy in my life. At this moment I am
not sitting in my favorite chair feeling sorry for myself;
instead, I am at my desk writing this brief chapter on a
great text in God's Word. Many times I have preached
from this text, but today I can testify that it is blessedly
true.

A Procedure

Our text then tells us that there is a procedure for coming to the throne of grace. We are to come "boldly." We dare not be brash or brazen, nor need we be bashful. We are urged to come "boldly." This word *boldly* means "confidently." We can speak freely and frankly to our Heavenly Father.

The high priest in Israel could enter the holy of holies only once a year, and then he had to stand silently before God. But something wonderful happened when Christ died on the cross. "And, behold, the veil of the temple was rent in twain from the top to the bottom" (Matthew 27:51). The believer in Christ now has access to what was once the place of exclusion. The apostle Paul declared that all of God's justified ones "have access by faith into this grace wherein we stand" (Romans 5:2).

We must never be shy about coming to this blessed place. We don't ever need to hesitate to tell God exactly what our need is. There are times when it is good for us to remain silent, but our time of need is not one of them. We are instructed to come boldly.

A Purpose

Hebrews 4:16 also teaches that there is a purpose for our coming to the throne of grace. And what is that purpose? ". . . that we may obtain mercy, and find grace to help in time of need."

Mercy is one of our primary needs because of our sins and failures. Our Heavenly Father is "the Father of mercies" (2 Corinthians 1:3), and He is "rich in mercy" (Ephesians 2:4). God's attitude toward those of His children who are in distress is one of mercy, pity, and compassion. In time of need we all appreciate someone who can empathize and sympathize with us. Will our loving God, who was merciful in saving us (Titus 3:5), be less merciful now that we are His children? Of course not!

Then let us go to Him with confidence and tell Him all about our need.

There are times when "we know not what we should pray for" (Romans 8:26). It is possible that you do not know what your needs are. But our Lord assures us that "your Father knoweth what things ye have need of, before ye ask him" (Matthew 6:8). See also Matthew 6:32.

A further purpose for our coming to the throne of grace is "to find grace to help." Mercy is for those failures of the past and grace is for the present hour of need.

The apostle Paul appeared before the throne of grace when he was suffering from his thorn in the flesh. Three times he asked God to remove this infirmity. But that was not what he needed. If he was suffering pain at that moment, it was perfectly natural for him to pray for relief from the discomfort. But at that moment of need he received this assuring word from the Lord: "My grace is sufficient for thee" (2 Corinthians 12:9). The Lord did not heal Paul, nor did He remove his discomfort at that time. But it was there—at the throne of grace—that he discovered the infinite, inexhaustible resource of God's grace. There he found grace for timely help. And that grace is available to you and me. "Let us therefore come boldly." God's grace sustains me even as I write these words.

A Person

Then too, we learn from Hebrews 4:16 that a Person is waiting to meet and greet us at the throne of grace. He is the Lord Jesus Christ, who died to redeem us from the guilt and penalty of our sins. Four times in this epistle to the Hebrews it is stated that He is at the right hand of the throne of God (1:3; 8:1; 10:12; 12:2). In another favorite portion of this same epistle, we are shown His three appearings: He did appear to redeem us (9;:26); He now appears to represent us (9:24); and He will appear to reward us (9:28). The teaching in Hebrews about the continuing ministry of our Lord Jesus Christ is precious indeed. His work in redeeming us is completed. His work in representing us continues. The one Person who is capable of meeting our total needs is now at the right hand of the throne of God. Let us come to Christ. The Bible tells us of three ways He works in our behalf.

He meets our need through His prayers. In his epistle to the Romans, the apostle Paul asked: Who is he that condemneth? It is Christ that died, yea rather, that is risen again, who is even at the right hand of God, who also maketh intercession for us (Romans 8:34). Christ is not condemning us; He is interceding for us. The author of Hebrews wrote, "He ever liveth to make intercession for them" (Hebrews 7:25). Therefore, let us come.

He meets our needs by His power. The throne of grace is the place of power, and our Lord Jesus Christ is the person of power. We see "the exceeding greatness of His power to usward who believe, according to the working of his mighty power, Which he wrought in Christ, when He raised him from the dead, and set him at his own right hand in the heavenly places" (Ephesians 1:19-20). Christ has an ability that knows no inability. Yes, He is able! He is able to save to the uttermost (Hebrews 7:25). He is able to keep us from falling (Jude 24). He is able to help those who are tempted (Hebrews 2:18). He is able to subdue all things (Philippians 3:21).

He meets our needs through His priesthood. While it is true that priesthood is as old as man, let us never lose sight of the fact that it is an institution of God. In Old Testament times the ministry of the priest was to appear before God in behalf of the children of Israel. This divine provision was an expression of the gracious compassion and concern of a holy God for His children. The priest was the Father's consecrated link between Himself and His own.

None but the Son of God Himself would qualify to be the great High Priest over the house of God.

> Seeing then that we have a great high priest, that is passed into the heavens, Jesus the Son of God let us hold fast our profession.
> For we have not an high priest which cannot be touched with the feeling of our infirmities; but was in all points tempted like as we are, yet without sin. (Hebrews 4:14-15)

Aaron's sons were priests; Aaron himself was a high priest; only the Lord Jesus Christ is our Great High Priest.

We know *where* He is—"passed into the heavens." We know *who* He is—"Jesus the Son of God." We know *what* He is—sinless. He is a sympathetic high priest. He does not sympathize with our sins but with our "infirmities." These infirmities are the sorrows, the sufferings, the sicknesses of this life. We know that our great High Priest is touched with the feeling of our infirmities.

If you are in need, come to Him now. No problem is too tough, no petition too trifling, and no power too transcendent for Him to handle. Let there be no lack of confidence between you and your great High Priest. He knows you. He loves you. He is waiting now for you to come to Him in your time of need.

The truth of this text is working for me right now. It will work for you. Do not delay in coming to God's throne of grace.

When troubles mount and pain increases, followers of Christ sometimes feel that they've been left to fight the battle alone. It can seem as though no one cares whether we are suffering or not; whether we are triumphant or we fail. And indeed, in the most intense moments of anguish, we may be almost beyond human help.

But we can take comfort and be encouraged by the sure, undeniable truth that God cares. The promise is clearly given in this wonderful verse: "Casting all your care upon him; for he careth for you" (1 Peter 5:7).

I found this out in a special way a few weeks after Elsie's illness began. As you read this chapter, may you become aware of the comforting truth that God cares!

5

He Cares

Life has its ups and downs, its highs and lows. At one time or another, every man and woman faces severe trial. Even the Christian in his most prosperous state cannot escape the testings and tribulations, the pains and pressures that are common to us all.

"Although affliction cometh not forth of the dust, neither doth trouble spring out of the ground; yet man is born unto trouble, as the sparks fly upward" (Job 5:6-7). Man's trials are not simply natural phenomena. Nothing occurs that is outside of the Creator's knowledge and purpose. "Man that is born of a woman is of few days, and full of trouble. He cometh forth like a flower, and is cut down: he fleeth also as a shadow, and continueth not" (Job 14:1-2).

The problems themselves often do not hurt the Christian nearly as much as the worry and anxiety that arise from them. Anxiety disturbs the Christian's mind and destroys his motivation. I was made aware of this fact as my Elsie entered the fifth week of her illness. It appeared for a while that she was making progress with the therapy, but then she developed pain in her left side, and the therapy was temporarily suspended. While driving home from the hospital that evening, I detected a twinge of anxiety coming upon me.

Almost immediately the Lord brought this verse to my mind: "Casting all your care upon him; for he careth for you" (1 Peter 5:7). Many were the times I had quoted that verse while preaching to others. I can remember saying with strong conviction to audiences, "He cares!" Then I would exhort them to cast all their cares upon Him.

Now I was facing the severest trial in my seventy-two years, and I freely confess to a bit of anxiety. Then the Holy Spirit flashed into my mind that great text from Peter's pen. I knew that every word was true, because God had given it to Peter. I quoted the verse aloud several times as I drove along. Then I sang a little chorus I had learned in 1927, about the time I was saved:

> He careth for you,
> He careth for you,
> Through sunshine or shadow,
> He careth for you.

When I arrived home from the hospital, I had the strong desire to meditate on Peter's famous and familiar verse. These are the thoughts I jotted down.

I noted that the exhortation was a vital part of a passage dealing with Christians who were suffering (4:12-19). Peter referred to those who "suffer according to the will of God" (4:19). The sovereign God had allowed severe trials to come to those believers in accordance with His own wise and perfect will. Therefore, they were urged to "commit the keeping of their souls to him." That means they could entrust the safety and security of their souls to God, their faithful Creator.

When we come to verse 7 of chapter 5, it is apparent

that their suffering was causing them some anxiety. They were beginning to worry. The word *care* in Greek is *merimna*, meaning "anxiety," or "a fearful and painful uneasiness of the mind." It is the crippling sin of worry that our Lord said chokes the Word so that it becomes unfruitful (Matthew 13:22). In my crisis hour, I certainly did not want to cut off the message and ministry of God's Word. That would have brought me a shameful defeat.

Paul had used the same word in its verb form when he wrote, "Be careful for nothing" (Philippians 4:6). He tells us not to worry about anything, for anxiety comes from not trusting God. Like Martha, at times we are "careful and troubled about many things" (Luke 10:41) when we should be anxious "for nothing." *Nothing means not even one thing!*

Peter told us what we are to do with all of our anxieties. We are to cast them upon our Lord. "Casting all your care upon Him." The Greek word for "cast" is *ballo*, which means "to deposit with" or "to commit." While it is not the same word translated "commit" in 1 Peter 4:19, it does contain the same thought. We are to take our painful anxieties and hurl them—all of them—on the Lord.

In spite of the sickness and sorrow that had come into our lives, I knew that Elsie and I could live carefree. Then and there I decided to cast all my anxieties on my blessed Lord. The heavy burden was lifted, and my heart had peace. Every Christian who is passing through a severe trial needs the experience of Peter's text. He must place his burden upon Christ.

If I worry, I am saying that God doesn't care. But the Scripture says He does care—"he careth for you." Coming back to this verse really gave me something to think about. The Word tells me that I am not to have care, and yet my Lord does care. Is this a contradiction? Of course not! The Bible never contradicts itself. The word *careth* in "he careth for you" is a different Greek word. It is *melei*, meaning that someone or something is the object of care— the object of attention, love, and thoughtfulness—rather than anxiety. Christians are the objects of God's love, and He therefore does care about us. Not that He is worried or anxious about us, but He does feel a personal interest in us. There is a difference between human anxiety and divine care.

In 1900, Frank Graeff wrote the following words. I have joined with others in singing them many times. Today I am singing them, but it is a solo.

> Does Jesus care when my heart is pained
>   Too deeply for mirth and song,
> As the burdens press, and the cares distress,
>   And the way grows weary and long?
>
> Does Jesus care when my way is dark
>   With a nameless dread and fear?
> As the daylight fades into deep night shades,
>   Does He care enough to be near?
>
> Oh yes, He cares—I know He cares!
>   His heart is touched with my grief;
> When the days are weary, the long nights dreary,
>   I know my Savior cares.

Today I have cast all my care upon my Lord. The psalmist said, "Cast thy burden upon the Lord, and he shall sustain thee: he shall never suffer the righteous to be moved" (Psalm 55:22). This psalm divides into three parts. Verses 1 through 8 express David's *complaint;* verses 9 through 15, David's *criticism;* verses 16 through 23, David's *confidence.* In the first section, David was thinking only of himself. In the second, his thoughts were against his enemies. In the third, he turned to God. It was when he turned to the Lord that he discovered God cares and that he could cast his burden upon Him. David was no braggart. He did not claim that he never worried. But he knew where to go with all his anxieties—he cast them upon the Lord.

Did you ever wonder if God really cares? When we

doubt that God cares, we insult Him. The disciples heaped a gross indignity upon our Lord when they said in the midst of the storm, "Master, carest thou not that we perish?" (Mark 4:38). Of course He cared. He had not said, "Let us set sail and be drowned." Rather, He had said, "Let us pass over unto the other side" (v. 35). The anxiety of the disciples showed that they were carrying their care instead of casting it on Him.

Think again about Martha, who was somewhat over-anxious about temporal provisions. She became wrapped up in the affairs of this world. She said to Jesus, "Lord, dost thou not care that my sister hath left me to serve alone?" (Luke 10:40). Of course He cared! He was more concerned about Martha than she was for herself. She was filled with sinful care, that anxiety that breeds self-pity. The Lord saw the disease that had fastened itself upon her woman's heart. "Martha, Martha," He said, "thou art careful and troubled about many things" (Luke 10:41). Martha had many admirable qualities, but she lacked the one thing she needed most. It was the quality her sister Mary possessed when she "sat at Jesus' feet, and heard his word" (Luke 10:39). Mary had no worry because she had cast it all upon Jesus.

Verse 40 says that "Martha was cumbered." The Greek word for "cumbered" is *perispao*, meaning "to be drawn away, to be distracted." Martha had a distracting anxiety that made her blind to the loving care of the Lord. She carried care with her that she could have cast on Christ. Her worry was a sin because it denied the love of the Lord Jesus.

Beloved, God has given us a remedy for the anxieties that arise from our trials. It is a distinctive characteristic of Christianity that the Lord Jesus Christ cares for those who put their trust in Him. The Christian can bring all of his anxieties to the Savior. "Casting *all* your care upon him; for he careth for you." Not some of them, or many of them, or most of them, but *all* of them. When we heed Peter's inspired exhortation, we do not throw off our trials and afflictions, but we do get rid of the worries they cause. The poet has written:

> It is His will that I should cast
>   My care on Him each day.
> He also bids me not to cast
>   My confidence away.
>
> But oh, how foolishly I act
> When taken unaware!
> I cast away my confidence
> And carry all my care.
>   (Author Unknown)

Yes, there is peace for the mind and comfort for the heart in knowing that my Savior cares for me. I have cast my care on Him, but if I worry I will be taking that care out of His hands. Yet I have decided that He is more able to handle it than I. Our Lord is no mere bystander or chance spectator watching us in our affliction. He is our great High Priest, and He is "touched with the feeling of our infirmities" (Hebrews 4:15). The Christian who is set free from anxiety is stronger to carry on the service to which God has called him. Worry is a contradiction to a life of trust. Anxiety has never done anything good for me, and it never will. By the grace and power of God, I hope to be done with faithless worry.

When I lived in the Philadelphia area, I became acquainted with the godly preacher Charles Tindley. The Christians knew him as Brother Tindley. He was both a gifted preacher of God's Word and a hymnwriter. Following is a part of his well-known hymn "Leave It There":

> If your body suffers pain
> And your health you can't regain,
>   And your soul is almost sinking in despair;
> Jesus knows the pain you feel,
> He can save and He can heal;
>   Take your burden to the Lord and leave it there.

When your youthful days are gone
And old age is stealing on,
  And your body bends beneath the weight of care;
He will never leave you then,
He'll go with you to the end;
  Take your burden to the Lord and leave it there.

Leave it there, leave it there,
Take your burden to the Lord and leave it there;
  If you trust and never doubt,
  He will surely bring you out;
Take your burden to the Lord and leave it there.

We know that feelings are changeable. They are affected by physical pain, by weariness, by need for sleep, by the suffering or death of a loved one. But beloved, our Lord cares. "For he knoweth our frame; he remembereth that we are dust" (Psalm 103:14). We must learn to roll every care upon Him. And when we do, we will discover that He can do infinitely more for us than we can do for ourselves. "Now unto him that is able to do exceeding abundantly above all that we ask or think, according to the power that worketh in us" (Ephesians 3:20).

In conclusion, let me leave you with two verses that I will expound later. "Be careful for nothing; but in everything by prayer and supplication with thanksgiving let your requests be made known unto God. And the peace of God, which passeth all understanding, shall keep your hearts and minds through Christ Jesus" (Philippians 4:6-7). Yes, our loving Lord cares!

God ever cares! Not only in life's summer
  When skies are bright and days are long and glad;
He cares as much when life is draped in winter,
  And heart feels so bereft, and lone, and sad.

God ever cares! His heart is ever tender,
  His love will never fail nor show decay;
The love of earth, though strong and deep, may perish,
  But His shall never, never pass away.

God ever cares! And thus when life is lonely,
  When blessings one time prized are growing dim,
The heart may find a sweet and sunny shelter—
  A refuge and a resting place in Him.

God ever cares! And time can never change Him.
  His nature is to care, and love, and bless;
And drearest, darkest, emptiest days afford Him
  The means to make more sweet His own caress.
                                    (Author Unknown)

The sovereign Lord is the great Provider. When Israel needed a leader, He raised up Moses. When they needed water in the desert, He supplied it from a rock. When they needed food for their wilderness wandering, He gave it in the form of manna. Man needed a Savior from his sins, so God sent His only begotten Son to die on Calvary's cross.

The hand of God's provision is also open to us in our time of affliction. He has provided for the need of His suffering saints. Paul wrote, "But my God shall supply all your need according to his riches in glory by Christ Jesus" (Philippians 4:19).

When we're deep in the vale of suffering, when we've been in God's waiting room for what seems like endless days, it may appear that the storehouse of God's supply is about to be exhausted. We may feel that He can do nothing more for us. But the promise of the Holy Scriptures is that He will supply all our need.

If you are in the valley of affliction, may you experience, as I have with my dear Elsie, the truth of this promise.

6

All You Need

One of many promises in the Bible that has strengthened and sustained God's children for centuries is Philippians 4:19: "But my God shall supply all your need according to His riches in glory by Christ Jesus." In this verse the apostle Paul was not introducing a new promise. The provision of God for His children had its roots deep in the Old Testament. In fact, it goes back to the very beginning of human history, when God created man and placed him in the Garden of Eden. There in the garden Adam and Eve had all they needed.

Our key text for this chapter, therefore, contains an old truth that needs to be recaptured by Christians today. The human source of supply has diverted our attention from God. With higher wages, social security, and guaranteed incomes for the unemployed, fewer people are bringing God into their thinking. In addition, some fine Christian men and women have never learned to trust God for all their needs.

Let us carefully examine Paul's text within its context. In an attitude of prayer, we will try to glean the lessons it has for our lives.

The Provider

The first important truth of Philippians 4:19 is that God is *the Provider*. The apostle said that the Lord is *"my God."* When Paul received the Lord Jesus on his way to Damascus, he was brought immediately into a personal relationship with God. I fear that the belief many persons have in the God of the Bible is merely intellectual and academic, not experiential. They believe God is omnipotent—that He has an ability that knows no inability—but they know nothing of a personal, intimate relationship with Him. Sometimes people inside our churches, as well as those outside, know about God, but they do not know Him. Paul knew Him as the provider of all his needs.

In the Old Testament the Hebrew name for God the provider is *Jehovah-jireh*. It appears in Genesis 22 when Abraham, in obedience to God's command, took his son Isaac to Mount Moriah to offer him for a burnt offering. After father and son had arrived at the designated place and prepared the altar, Isaac said to his father, "Behold the fire and the wood: but where is the lamb for a burnt offering? And Abraham said, My son, God will provide himself a lamb for a burnt offering" (Genesis 22:7-8). And that is precisely what God did: He provided a substitute to die in the place of Isaac (v. 13). "And Abraham called the name of that place Jehovah-jireh" (v. 14), meaning "the Lord will provide." But keep this fact in mind: Abraham did not experience God's miraculous provision without first giving obedience to God's command. Abraham was not presumptuous; rather, he displayed implicit faith and obedience. He became acquainted with *Jehovah-jireh*.

Do you know who *Jehovah-jireh* is? He is the God who provides. He is the God of the Bible, and the God and Father of our Lord Jesus Christ. It is through personal faith in Christ that we gain that experiential knowledge of God. Jesus said, "I am the way, the truth, and the life: no man cometh unto the Father, but by me" (John 14:6). Can you say with the apostle that Jehovah-jireh is "my God"?

The Promise

The second important truth in Philippians 4:19 is found in this promise: "My God *shall* supply." Take note of how this thought follows logically upon the first. The expression "my God," used also by Paul in Philippians 1:3, gives assurance that one who is rightly related to God will have his needs supplied. There is to be no doubting, no hesitation, no apprehension. Our Lord said, "Ask, and it *shall* be given you; seek, and ye *shall* find; knock, and it *shall* be opened unto you" (Matthew 7:7). "And all things, whatsoever ye shall ask in prayer, believing, ye *shall* receive" (Matthew 21:22). There is positive assurance in these promises.

Why can a believer be confident that his need will be supplied? Because the promise is supported by the Provider. "My God" is the all-knowing Provider; therefore, He knows exactly what I need. Twice in one discourse our Lord said, "your Father knoweth what things ye have need of, before ye ask Him" (Matthew 6:8). "For your heavenly Father knoweth that ye have need of all these things" (v. 32). In contrast with God's omniscience is our lack of knowledge. The apostle Paul reminded us that "we know not what we should pray for as we ought" (Romans 8:26). Because we are inherently selfish, our prayer requests often reflect more greed than need. As I think back over the years, I am thankful that God did not grant my selfish requests.

The writer to the Hebrews was commenting on this truth when he wrote, "For ye have need of patience, that, after ye have done the will of God, ye might receive the promise" (Hebrews 10:36). I know that it is not God's will for me to be impatient, yet I must admit that I have been woefully lacking in patience. Perseverance has never been one of my strong points. I have been in need of patience throughout most of my Christian experience, spanning more than fifty-five years. For at least thirty of those years I never once prayed that God would supply that need. However, God knew what I needed. To say it as Jesus said it, "your Father knoweth what things ye have need of."

There were times when I was baffled about why trials and tribulations had come my way. I would ask God to remove the trial, believing that was what I needed, when my real need was patience. Then I learned that God had sent the trial, because it was His way of producing patience. If this boggles your mind, perhaps the Word of God will make it clear to you. "My brethren, count it all joy when ye fall into divers trials, knowing this, that the trying of your faith worketh patience" (James 1:2-3). The *Provider* keeps his *promise* to supply all our need. I am satisfied that He knows my need and that He keeps His promise.

The Provision

Third, let us examine the *provision* spoken of in Philippians 4:19. The apostle summed it up in three words, "all your need." Not *some* of your need, not *much* of your need, nor *most* of your need, but *all* of your need. That is bountiful provision! God can meet the many and varied needs of His children because of His infinite and inestimable riches.

The psalmist prayed, "O Lord, how manifold are thy works! in wisdom hast thou made them all: the earth is full of thy riches" (Psalm 104:24). Notice that it is the earth which is full of God's riches, and it is on the earth where God has put us. The psalmist linked man and God's riches together when he wrote, "The earth is the Lord's, and the fulness thereof; the world, and they who dwell therein" (Psalm 24:1).

The apostle Paul quoted this verse from the Psalms

twice. He did this to remind us that the earth and everything in it belongs to the Lord (1 Corinthians 10:26, 28). The Lord Himself said, "For every beast of the forest is mine, and the cattle upon a thousand hills. I know all the fowls of the mountains: and the wild beasts of the field are mine. If I were hungry, I would not tell thee: for the world is mine, and all the fulness thereof" (Psalm 50:10-12). Our great Provider created and controls all of the provision.

How vast is the wealth of God? How rich is the Provider? I doubt that we will ever fully know in this life the extent of God's riches. He said to His people Israel, "And I will give thee the treasures of darkness, and hidden riches of secret places, that thou mayest know that I, the Lord, which call thee by thy name, am the God of Israel" (Isaiah 45:3). Yes, God has hidden riches in secret places about which we know nothing. The apostle Paul mentioned "the riches of his goodness" (Romans 2:4), "the riches of his glory" (Romans 9:23; Ephesians 3:16), and "the riches of his grace" (Ephesians 1:7; 2:7). What an amazing provision!

We Christians who read the Bible know all of this, and we know that it is all true. But do we show plainly and clearly from day to day that we live in that personal knowledge of God and His bountiful provision for us? If we do, we need never be anxious, and we must never be worried. If we would really and truly grasp the truth of this great text, then worry, stress, and anxiety would be banished from our lives. In other words, we must bring ourselves in mind and heart and will to take seriously what our Heavenly Father says to us. We must exercise ourselves to rely implicitly upon His Word. We are never alone in our need. We always have access to the Provider and His provision.

The Plentitude

Next, Paul spoke of the plentitude of God's supply. He gives to His children "according to his riches in glory by Christ Jesus." God's giving is not merely from His riches, or out of His riches, but according to His riches. Suppose you have an urgent and a legitimate need for $1,000 and I have $100,000 in my savings account. We have been friends for a long time. You come to me and tell me about your need. Without hesitating, I write a check in your name in the amount of $100. I would be giving to you *out of* my riches, but not *according to* my riches. And because my giving was so meager, your need would not be supplied. If I were to give to you according to my riches, however, I would write out the check for $1,000—and your need would be supplied.

God has promised to supply our need *according* to His riches. This tells us that we cannot have a need too great for God to supply. Our Heavenly Father knows what our need is, and all His riches are made available to His own. "He that spared not his own Son, but delivered him up for us all, how shall he not with him also freely give us all things?" (Romans 8:32). God, who gave His own beloved Son to redeem us and make us His children, will not refuse to meet our needs. God has underwritten the supply of our every need. He has given His word. Christian friend, let us never question or doubt this great truth. God's unlimited supply and His unfailing word should satisfy our minds now and for all of time. God's wealth is at our disposal, and this is a provision beyond calculation. Don't impoverish yourself by refusing to take God at His word. You are His personal property, and He desires to give you His perpetual care.

The words "in glory" have caused a problem for some believers. They interpret them to mean that all our needs will be supplied in the glorious ages of the future—not the present. Personally, I do not believe that Paul was referring here to a future age. The promise in our text refers to the present life—to material and bodily needs as well as to spiritual needs. It speaks of "all" of them; that is, to every one of our needs. The whole context of this passage in Philippians 4 is in reference to the needs of this life. In verse 16, Paul spoke of his personal need, which was most certainly a need he had at that time. No one will argue against the idea that our total needs will be supplied in heaven. Quite frankly, I do not believe that we shall have any needs in heaven.

Don't miss the blessing of our text by pushing its promise into a future time. The *New International Version* translates the text as follows: "And my God will meet all your needs according to his glorious riches in Christ Jesus." Lenski suggests the possibility that it means "in a glorious manner"; that is, that "God will gloriously supply every need." Whatever the case, Paul was obviously telling his readers that God would supply their needs in the here and now. I am convinced that he was speaking of this life, not the next.

Read our Lord's teaching on this subject in Matthew 6:19-34. He was talking about the material needs of this life—finances, food, fashions, and our earthly future. He used the word "money" in verse 24, a word that represents the material and mundane things of this life. And then He added, "For your heavenly Father knoweth that ye have need of all these things" (v. 32). Philippians 4:19 promises God's abundant supply for our daily needs in this life.

The Prerequisite

A fifth and final thought must not be overlooked. Some *prerequisites* must be met before we can receive God's provision. It is not mentioned in the text itself. You will not find it in verse 19. But it is there in the context, particularly in verse 18. The two verses are linked with the word *but*, a conjunction that ties them together.

Beginning at verse 14, the apostle reminded the Christians at Philippi of the generosity they had shown him in his need. He said, "ye did communicate with my affliction." Paul elaborated further on this in the next verse, telling them that "no church communicated with me as concerning giving and receiving, but ye only" (v. 15). In both verses he used the word *communicate.* If we want to claim the promise and provision in verse 19, we dare not gloss over these verses lightly. There is implicit teaching here, and if we fail to pay attention to it we will miss the blessing. Why is it that so many believers tend to say, "I am a Christian. I believe Philippians 4:19, but it doesn't work for me"? In all probability, those Christians have not carefully examined verses 14 through 18.

The Philippian believers had shared generously with the apostle in the ministry God had entrusted to him. Their giving was not casual, nor did they give only when it was convenient for them. We know this because he reminded them in verse 16, "For even in Thessalonica ye sent once and again unto my necessity." Paul rejoiced in their giving, not because of what it did for him, but because of what it did for them. Their giving had actually added to their account (v. 17). The motive, manner, and measure of their giving had a definite and direct effect on their being able to claim the promise of verse 19. Because they were in good standing with God the Provider, this gave to them the right to claim His promise. There is no need to argue this point; it is the obvious truth.

All this can be seen in verse 18. Notice how Paul described their gifts: "an odour of a sweet smell, a sacrifice acceptable, wellpleasing to God." Here the apostle was clinching his main argument, namely, that if God is not pleased with our giving, then we have no claim upon Him. The expression "an odour of a sweet smell [or savor]" is an Old Testament phrase for a sacrifice that pleased God. The term was used frequently in a symbolic sense. If the offering displeased God, it was a "stinking savour" (Ecclesiastes 10:1), or a "stink" (Joel 2:20). But when God was pleased, it was called "a sweet savour" (Genesis 8:21; Exodus 29:18; Leviticus 1:9, 13, 17; 2:9; 3:5; 16; 4:31). The Christians at Philippi gave sacrificially out of a pure motive; therefore, the apostle could say to them, "My God shall supply all your need."

This is the essential lesson in our Lord's teaching to

His disciples in Matthew 6:19-34. Let me make this point again. Christ talked about their need for money, food, drink, clothing, and shelter, and He assured them that their heavenly Father knew that they needed all those things (6:32). But the mere fact that God knew of their needs was not in itself a guarantee that they would receive what they needed. Such knowledge about God might relieve any of us of worry, stress, and anxiety. But merely knowing God as the omniscient provider is not sufficient.

What is the prerequisite to a valid claim upon God for our total needs? Our Lord said, "But seek ye first the kingdom of God, and his righteousness; and all these things shall be added unto you" (Matthew 6:33). Jesus did not speak these words to unbelievers in order to tell them how to become believers. He was telling believers how they could lay hold of all the necessities of life. "His disciples came unto him: And he ... taught them" (Matthew 5:1-2). He was telling them how to behave as children of God. They would have needs in their lives. Those needs were known to God. But if those needs were to be supplied, the disciples would have to put first things first. So He said to them, and to us, "Seek ye first the kingdom of God, and his righteousness, and all these things shall be added unto you."

Pursue holiness. Behave rightly. This is what pleases God. It is what moves Him to supply all our needs. The more righteous we are in our behavior, the nearer we are to God's storehouse. "Blessed are they which do hunger and thirst after righteousness: for they shall be filled" (Matthew 5:6). If you put God and your relationship to Him first, then you have His pledge that all your needs will be supplied.

We must first understand this truth. Then we must take the initial step and pursue it each day. Don't put the other things first, but put God first. We have no right to pray, "Give us this day our daily bread" (6:11) until we "seek ... first the kingdom of God, and His righteousness" (6:33). This is the same prerequisite that the apostle Paul was talking about in Philippians 4.

Truth explained is a far cry from truth experienced. The following chapter is from a message I prepared some time ago for the blessing and benefit of others.

Romans 8:28 was one of many verses Elsie and I claimed after her stroke, and we have repeated it often. When I was preparing this message, I did not have the slightest idea that God was going to use it in my own life. But our heavenly Father knew what lay ahead for me. Now I know much more about the real meaning of this text. That is because my knowledge is not only intellectual and academic, but it is also now experiential.

The text does not tell us how God works all things together for good—only that He does. With that assurance, no matter how deep the valley or how severe the trial, I will not doubt God's Word.

One day our Lord said, "What I do thou knowest not now; but thou shalt know hereafter" (John 13:7). My heavenly Father is sovereign, all-wise, and all-powerful, and He is in control of "all things." He will accomplish His perfect will through our trials. And in His own time, He will show us how it worked for good.

7

A Soft Pillow
for Troubled Hearts
and Suffering Bodies

One of the most quoted passages in the Bible is Romans 8:28-29.

> And we know that all things work together for good to them that love God, to them who are the called according to His purpose.
> For whom He did foreknow, He also did predestinate to be conformed to the image of His Son, that He might be the firstborn among many brethren.

Where is there a Christian who has not heard it, in part at least? I would not conclude that all those persons who recite Romans 8:28 from time to time know and understand its meaning. Nevertheless, the frequency with which we hear it gives evidence that many at least know this verse is in the Bible.

This text is a part of a passage that speaks about the "sufferings of this present time" (8:18). All creation is said to be groaning (8:19-22). The Christian himself is groaning (8:23-25), and even the Holy Comforter "maketh intercession for us with groanings which cannot be uttered" (8:26).

Problems and pressures are felt in all areas of life. Tears, trials, and tribulations are seen on every hand. Most of us will admit that this is true. Of course, some persons live in a world of make-believe and say that such conclusions are merely "mind over matter." These people, I sincerely believe, are victims of satanic deception.

Despite the infirmities of life, however, no Christian needs to fear or live a life of defeat. Our text provides a soft pillow for troubled hearts and suffering bodies. We are assured that all of life's hardships and heartaches and heavy burdens are working "together for good to them that love God, to them who are the called according to His purpose." Here we see the providence of God at work. Here we learn that we must never think about "chance" or "luck" regarding those things that touch our lives.

As we examine the words of Romans 8:28, we discover five distinct emphases. Each of them is necessary to an understanding of the whole meaning of this wonderful passage of promise.

The Positiveness Involved

The text commences on a positive note: "We know." The word *know, oida,* means "to know with an absolute knowledge." It is not something we blindly accept merely because someone says it. This is knowledge gained by looking back, by the mental process of reflection.

There are some things about our lives that we do not know now. The passage of Scripture that forms the setting for our text says that "we know not what we should pray for as we ought" (Romans 8:26). Our Lord said, "Watch therefore: for ye know not what hour your Lord doth come" (Matthew 24:42). Then, just before His ascension, He added, "It is not for you to know the times or the seasons, which the Father hath put in his own power" (Acts 1:7). We all must say with the apostle, "Now I know in part" (1 Corinthians 13:12). Yes, in regard to many things, our vision and understanding are limited.

But Romans 8:28 tells us one thing we can know absolutely. This verse has become a household word among those who love God; a thing known by those who are "the called according to His purpose." So at once we rule out fate or chance as a force in human events. We may not be able to explain satisfactorily just how all things work together for good, but we know that they do. This knowledge comes through reflection and through faith in the Word of God. We know it because God said it. He has guaranteed it by His character. And if someone reading these lines is wondering how a rational person, knowing the grim facts of this world's present state, can make such a statement, I can only answer with confidence that I believe God.

Whenever God declares Himself, we are very foolish to doubt His Word. No obstacle or opposition is powerful enough to prevent Him from carrying out His plan. Consider the case of Abraham. God had told the aged patriarch that he was to become the father of a son, and that Sarah would be the child's mother. Humanly speaking, the odds were against them—so much so that Sarah laughed at the Lord's prediction. Then God asked, "Is anything too hard for the Lord?" (Genesis 18:14). Why, of course not!

If God says it will be done, then it will be done. His Word will settle it in our minds once and for all, and we must reply confidently, "There is nothing too hard for thee" (Jeremiah 32:17). When God says that all things work together for good to them that love Him, we accept it in faith.

Not one of us knows how long he will live. Not one of us knows whether the years ahead will be spent in sickness or in health. None of us knows if tragedy will strike in the home. None of us knows if America will be spared from falling into the hands of communism. None of us knows if our beloved nation will be involved in a nuclear war. None of us knows if our national economy will survive or collapse. But this we do know: that *all things* (not some things, or many things, or most things, but *all things*) continue to work together for good to those who love God. Nothing is more necessary to the Christian's peace of mind than the absolute knowledge that all things of every description that touch his life are overruled by God for his good.

But in order that no one be led into a false security, we must examine the text further and see who is the subject in this verse.

The People Involved

To whom is this assuring word addressed? It is to "them that love God." Up to this point the apostle has been speaking about God's love for us (Romans 5:5, 8). But here the change appears, and it is an important one. It is important because mankind believes the lie that as long as God loves us, all will be well and ultimate good will come to us. This is not so! In this verse it is not the question of God's love for us, but of our love toward Him. We may be certain that God has never stopped loving mankind; nevertheless, we must remember that all the people who will go to hell will not be there because God did not love them. "If any man love not the Lord Jesus Christ, let him be Anathema" (1 Corinthians 16:22).

Likewise, all Christians are loved by God, but only those whose hearts are right toward Him can claim the promised blessing in our text. I submit to you, then, that the phrase "them that love God" does not refer to all believers but to a certain class of believers. All Christians are being loved by God at all times (Revelation 1:5), but not all whom He loves choose to love Him in return. Our Lord said to the church at Ephesus, "I have somewhat against thee, because thou hast left thy first love" (Revelation 2:4). Three times Christ explored Peter's heart with the searching question, "Lovest thou me?" (John 21:15-17).

Who are these Christians who love God? They are those who live in daily fellowship with Him, who walk with Him in trust and obedience. Our Lord said, "If ye love me, keep my commandments" (John 14:15). On another occasion, He said that the first and great commandment is to "love the Lord thy God with all thy heart, and with all thy soul, and with all thy mind" (Matthew 22:37). There can be no doubt that faith in God and obedience to God are the real proofs of our love for Him. If a Christian loves and trusts God, then he will humbly accept all that God sends into his life. But if a Christian does not love and trust God, he will most likely resent the bitter trials of life.

The people involved are further described as "them who are the called according to His purpose." The called ones are not all those who were evangelized and invited, but those who obeyed the call and came to Christ, and who love and serve Him. The called, then, are the "effectually called," those who have responded to the call. By this they have accepted the blessings of the gospel which are for those who are in Christ.

Let's now consider a third factor in Romans 8:28.

The Particulars Involved

What percentage of those things that touch the Christian are working together for his good? The answer is "all things." This means *all of them*—without exception! A striking example of this is the case of Paul himself, the man who penned these words from God. Before his conversion, he had initiated a bitter persecution against the Christians. Although it caused the congregation of believers from Jerusalem to scatter to other parts of the world, this seeming calamity served only for the good of Christ's cause. The church was planted in scores of new places to prosper in its mission more than ever (Acts 8). When God

says all things, He means all things, whatever they may
be, including persecution. No limitations are placed on
the particulars involved.

Consider the case of Paul's thorn in the flesh (2 Corinthians 12:7-10). This was most certainly a severe trial to
him. Three times he had prayed, asking God to remove
that particular affliction. No doubt he thought sincerely
that it was a hindrance to him in his work of the gospel.
But Paul had to learn, as each of us does, that God doesn't
need human strength and physical well-being.

I have wondered at times if Paul, just before that
experience of suffering, was not building up within him a
bit of pride in his accomplishments and in the special
revelations God had given him. When he wrote by inspiration concerning his suffering, he said, "And lest I should
be exalted above measure through the abundance of the
revelations, there was given to me a thorn in the flesh, the
messenger of Satan to buffet me, lest I should be exalted
above measure" (2 Corinthians 12:7). Notice that twice he
said, "Lest I should be exalted above measure." The trial,
therefore, was for the purpose of preventing pride. This
was for the good of God's servant, because "pride goeth
before destruction, and an haughty spirit before a fall"
(Proverbs 16:18).

Of course, Paul could not see the good in his tribulation when he was on his knees begging God to take it from
him. Even so, it was working for his good. He did see it
afterward, for he testified, "Therefore, I take pleasure in
infirmities, in reproaches, in necessities, in persecutions,
in distresses for Christ's sake: for when I am weak, then
am I strong" (2 Corinthians 12:10).

Then too, the apostle learned the sufficiency of God's
grace in the hour of suffering. Yes, when God says all
things, He means all things, including pain and physical
handicap. No limitations are placed on the particulars
involved.

Think also about the case of Joseph. His own brothers
had conspired against him. Their hearts were filled with

the awful evil of jealousy, and they sold him as a slave to the Ishmaelites for twenty pieces of silver. He was then taken to Egypt. During the years that followed, while Joseph's brothers did not know of his whereabouts, he was elevated to the official position of governor in Egypt. Many years later, when Joseph was united with his brothers, he testified, "But as for you, ye thought evil against me; but God meant it unto good, to bring to pass, as it is this day, to save much people alive" (Genesis 50:20). Yes, my Christian brethren, when God says all things He means all things, including misunderstanding and ill-treatment by our very own loved ones. There are no limitations on the particulars involved.

Further light is shed upon the subject as we examine the process God uses.

The Process Involved

We are told in our key verse that "all things work together for good." Now, nowhere does the text state that all things are good; but rather, that all things work together for good. Whatever the particulars involved may be, whether pain, poverty, persecution, misunderstanding, or death, they are not good in themselves. The idea is that God by His own supernatural processes intermingles all things in our lives for ultimate good. To state it another way, God makes each thing in our lives contribute to the good, for He is controlling the process. Only He knows the end from the beginning. Thus the bitter elements of life as well as the sweet blend together to produce the desired result.

Please look again at that word *together*, for it is the key to understanding the process involved. The isolated experience itself is not what accomplishes the result. It is that experience added to every other experience and their working together that produces the good. When I was a boy, I enjoyed watching Mother make a cake. First she would gather all the necessary ingredients for the cake.

There would be the flour, baking powder, shortening, sugar, raw eggs, and extract for flavoring. Taken by itself, any one of those ingredients would be unpalatable. Have you ever tried eating a bowl of flour or a cup of shortening or a spoonful of baking powder? Any one of those ingredients eaten by itself would not taste good, but when they are properly intermingled and baked at the right temperature for the correct number of minutes, the finished product is delicious.

The experience of those who love God is that all things intermingle for good. You may not be very old, and yet you can look back on life and see that some things seemed to be disastrous, but they worked out to your edification and blessing. God's guiding hand was in it all. If we love God, all things, however contrary they may appear, are under His control for our good. Suffering and sorrow, trials and troubles do not hinder our spiritual progress; rather, they serve to carry out the plan of God for us. They are part of the course in God's school of grace, given to us that we might learn His ways.

David said with confidence in God, "It is good for me that I have been afflicted: that I might learn thy statutes" (Psalm 119:71). He was simply saying that all things, including his affliction, worked together for good. The good in his case was acquiring a greater knowledge of the ways and will of God. This is the divine process, and it cannot fail. Most things in the process of making do not bear the slightest resemblance to the finished product. Therefore, do not be disillusioned by the process involved. You can be certain that all of the parts are being intermingled by Him, and that they will produce a good and glorious finished product.

We conclude this look at our text with a final thought.

The Purpose Involved

The text tells us that it is "His purpose" that we should be "conformed to the image of his Son" (Romans

8:29). The purpose of God will eventually be realized in all Christians. This will happen when Christ comes, and "we shall all be changed" (1 Corinthians 15:51-52) and "be like him" (1 John 3:2). God set this goal for His children before the worlds were made. I do not believe that Romans 8:28 was intended to be an expression of philosophy or theology; rather, it was meant to be an expression of Christian experience. How tragic that so many have read into this passage the lie that God predestinates people to go to hell! *He does no such thing.* As a matter of fact, God has predestined all of His children to be conformed to the image of Jesus Christ. He wants us to be sons after the pattern of Christ. This is God's settled plan and purpose for all believers, and this is the way it will be when our Lord comes for His own (Philippians 3:21).

Even so, God wants Christ's likeness to be seen in us now. The point is that all things work together for good here and now to them that love Him, so that in *this life* the image of God's Son may be manifest in us. The moral character of Christ is to be manifest in believers now. We must not wait until the conformity is fully and finally accomplished in the rapture. The purpose of the process of sanctification is for the present life as well as for the life to come.

God has set limits or boundaries upon His people. For the Christian, certain things are out of bounds because they detract from the likeness of Christ in us by hindering the work of conformation. Conformation to the image of the Lord Jesus begins the moment a sinner is saved. It is the work of the Holy Spirit in us through the process called sanctification.

If we love the Lord as we ought to love Him, we should say with a glad heart, "Work on, O God! Blend all things together, the bitter with the sweet, until You have made me like the Lord Jesus Christ."

The believer in Christ is expected to get to know God better as he walks the pilgrim pathway. But there are things that he can learn only through suffering. One of those things is that He is the God of all comfort.

I had known throughout my ministry, of course, that God comforts His own. I had taught about the ministry of the Holy Spirit, our paraclete, who was sent by Christ to help us. And I had seen that the reading of the Bible brings solace to sorrowing hearts and peace to those in great turmoil.

But now my wife and I are experiencing God's comfort for ourselves. In the months since Elsie's stroke, we have known daily the comfort of the Savior, the indwelling Holy Spirit, and the precious Word of God. May you too learn for yourself, in your day of trial, that the Lord is truly the God of all comfort.

8

The God
of All Comfort

The faith of the Christian should grow stronger in times of trial and trouble. Trials have a way of digging up the soil of our hearts and turning up weeds. That is good for us, for it is not in the sunshine but in the storm that we discover the depth of our need. Someone has said, "Great soldiers are not made in the barracks nor on the parade ground, but on the battlefield where the going is tough."

Trials provide opportunities for us to get to know God better. In his epistle to the Colossians, Paul assured the Christians that he was praying for them on a regular basis. Included in the list of things for which he prayed was the request that they might be "increasing in the knowledge of God" (Colossians 1:10). Paul knew that one of the secrets to a full and blessed life is getting to know God better.

The primary source of the knowledge of God is His Word. The book of Proverbs says, "My son, if thou wilt receive my words, and lay up my commandments with

thee. . . . Then shalt thou understand the fear of the Lord,
and find the knowledge of God" (Proverbs 2:1, 5). As every
student of the Bible knows, God does reveal Himself in
His Word.

We may discover God in other areas of life as well.
Psalm 46 begins with the following words: "God is our
refuge and strength, a very present help in trouble." As we
approach the end of the psalm, God is speaking and He
says, "Be still, and know that I am God" (v. 10). Times of
trouble are very often times of silence. At least we are sure
that days filled wih suffering and sorrow give us the opportunity to be silent. These can be precious moments of
quiet reflection when God speaks to us. If we do not set
aside some time each day to be silent before God, then He
has His own way of setting us aside. If we take advantage
of these periods of quiet solitude, we too can increase in
the knowledge of God. Yes, dear friends, our time of trouble can be for each of us a time of getting to know God
better.

In the lengthy but lovely 119th Psalm, David gave his
personal testimony of something he learned about God
when he was afflicted. In this one psalm, the word *afflicted*
occurs four times (vv. 67, 71, 75, 107), and the word
affliction three times (vv. 50, 92, 153). In each of those
seven verses, the psalmist spoke of himself and the affliction he suffered, but not once did he complain or find
fault with God. Here is a suggested outline as I look at
these verses in the order in which they appear:

> Divine Provision in Affliction (v. 50)
> Divine Prevention in Affliction (v. 67)
> Divine Purpose in Affliction (v. 71)
> Divine Providence in Affliction (v. 75)
> Divine Protection in Affliction (v. 92)
> Definite Prayer in Affliction (vv. 107, 153)

This is neither the time nor the occasion to expound on all
of these six points, so let me briefly draw your attention

to just two of them. In verse 71, the psalmist said, "It is good for me that I have been afflicted; that I might learn thy statutes." He considered God's school of affliction to be a learning place. There he learned, among other lessons, that God has a purpose in sending affliction to His children. In his first use of the noun *affliction*, the psalmist said, "This is my comfort in my affliction: for thy word quickened me" (v. 50). As he sat silently before God in his affliction, he learned by personal experience that God is the God of all comfort.

Comfort in affliction and adversity. That is the theme of this meditation. Three months after Elsie was afflicted with her stroke, neither her brain nor her body was functioning normally. The stroke has left her with brain impairment, and with paralysis on the left side of her body. She also has other problems: impaired vision, change in the pitch of her voice, and excessive fatigue are just a few of the side effects.

After spending seventy-seven consecutive days with Elsie in the hospital room, I knew full well that we were facing the severest trial in our fifty-one years of marriage. For forty-five of those years, I had been preaching and teaching the Word of God to others. Never once did I doubt the truths I was called of God to declare, but I must confess that I had never experienced much of what I preached and taught. But now God was giving me an opportunity to prove His Word to be gloriously and wondrously true.

One of the key passages in 2 Corinthians is greatly needed today. As a matter of fact, there never has been a time when it was not needed. It is at once both timely and timeless. Let us look together at this brief portion of two verses:

> Blessed be God, even the Father of our Lord Jesus Christ, the Father of mercies, and the God of all comfort;
> Who comforteth us in all our tribulation, that we may be able to comfort them who are in any trouble, by the

comfort with which we ourselves are comforted of God.
(2 Corinthians 1:3-4)

When Paul spoke of *the God of all comfort,* he was speaking of a knowledge of God that he himself had experienced. Undoubtedly he included himself in the plural word
"us" in verse 4. I take this as his personal testimony that
in all of his troubles and tribulations, he was comforted
by God. That comfort did not merely enable him to endure his trials but also to receive special blessings from
them. Paul's knowledge of God as *the God of all comfort* is
therefore not a mere intellectual and academic one; it is a
blessed and rewarding experience. He knows what he is
talking about. He suffered such severe tribulation in Asia
that he even despaired of his life (1:8-9).

In no way can my small trial be compared with the
severity of Paul's many encounters with suffering. But I
have prayed that the Holy Spirit will use this meditation
as a testimony to the effectiveness of those Scriptures in
our lives since Elsie had her stroke. *The God of all comfort*
has been sustaining and strengthening us day by day. He
has relieved the painful pressures so that we are able to
bear them without losing heart.

The word *comfort* comes from the Greek word *paraklēsis.* It appears ten times in verses 3 through 7, and is
translated "comfort" six times and "consolation" four times.
It combines the idea of solace with soothing.

Paraklēsis is made up of *para* meaning "beside," and
kaleo meaning "to call." The Christian who is suffering
needs a special kind of comfort that only God can give. As
our loving Comforter, He stands by our side to minister
the soothing balm we need.

Linked with the description of God as the God of all
comfort is the statement that He is *the Father of mercies.*
'Mercy is the outward manifestation of compassion for
others in their affliction. Mercy had its origin with God,
who is called its Father. All acts of pity and compassion
proceed from Him. God has a tender feeling of compas-

sion for us when we are in distress. Our trials, however slight or severe, have His attention. David expressed it as follows: "Like as a father pitieth his children, so the Lord pitieth them that fear him. For he knoweth our frame; he remembereth that we are dust" (Psalm 103:13-14). When we are being tested by adversity and affliction, compassion flows to us from His great loving heart. We never need to fear that His supply of mercy will run out, because He is "rich in mercy" (Ephesians 2:4).

God showed his mercy by providing for our eternal salvation, for it was "according to his mercy he saved us" (Titus 3:5). In another epistle, Paul wrote, "He that spared not his own Son, but delivered him up for us all, how shall he not with him also freely give us all things?" (Romans 8:32). One of the "all things" is His comfort.

"All things . . . all comfort." The word *all* in the Greek is a strong word. It means "every kind, every variety, the whole of, or the totality of the thing referred to."[1]

God's comfort is unique. It is infinite, inexhaustible, immutable, and indestructible. Our afflictions are temporary and transient; God's comfort is "everlasting" (2 Thessalonians 2:16). It is available at all times."

No Christian is left to face sickness and sorrow alone. God said to His children in Israel, "As one whom his mother comforteth, so will I comfort you" (Isaiah 66:13). The Israelites needed to be reminded of God's love and pity for them when He redeemed them from Egyptian bondage. Isaiah also wrote, "In all their affliction he [God] was afflicted, and the angel of his presence saved them: in his love and in his pity he redeemed them; and he bore them, and carried them all the days of old" (Isaiah 63:9).

Some Christians are prone to forget how real and precious God's love and comfort were when they received the Lord Jesus Christ as Savior. Friend, your heavenly

1. W.E. Vine, *Expository Dictionary of the New Testament* (Nashville: Thomas Nelson, 1978), pp. 46-47.

Father does care, and He does comfort. Turn to Him and give Him the privilege of ministering to your need. You are His child, and He is there when you hurt.

Let us now take a look at some of the divinely provided means of comfort, ways by which God's comfort comes to us.

First there is the comfort of the Savior. When our Lord Jesus Christ was on earth, He was the Comforter to His disciples. He was alongside to sustain them when they were drifting on the storm-tossed sea. He was alongside to supply for them when there was a shortage of food. He was alongside to strengthen them when they suffered persecution at the hands of their enemies. He was alongside to solace them in their sorrows. He was the divine *paraclete*.

The Greek word *paraclete* is translated "advocate" in 1 John 2:1. "My little children, these things write I unto you, that ye sin not. And if any man sin, we have an advocate with the Father, Jesus Christ the righteous." The word *advocate* is the same Greek word translated "comforter."

You see, our Lord's death did not bring to an end His ministry of comfort for His own. He arose from death and the grave, and He ascended to heaven, where He is now at the Father's right hand on our behalf. He is there to represent us, even when we sin. Not that He asks for leniency, nor that He approves of our sin. But He is there as the One who fulfilled every demand of the law by His sinless life and substitutionary death on our behalf. What a blessed Comforter is our Lord Jesus Christ!

The apostle Paul spoke about the present ministry of Christ for His own in his epistle to the Romans. "Who is he that condemneth? Is it Christ that died, yea rather, that is risen again, who is even at the right hand of God; who also maketh intercession for us" (Romans 8:34). Paul knew much about "the sufferings of this present time" (Romans 8:18). Never once did he deny that Christians would face adversity and affliction. But he did assure us that the Christian who is called to suffer has a Comforter in the person of the Lord Jesus Christ.

By His death Christ removed the guilt and penalty of our sin; by His resurrection from death He gives eternal life to every person who trusts Him for salvation; in His ascension and exaltation to the Father He intercedes for us. He does now "appear in the presence of God for us" (Hebrews 9:24), where "he ever liveth to make intercession for [us]" (Hebrews 7:25). He is "touched with the feeling of our infirmities" (Hebrews 4:15), not merely theoretically but practically. When He was here on earth, Jesus knew what it was to be hungry and thirsty. He suffered physically. He wept because of the sins and sorrows of others.

Our great High Priest understands, and He ministers in our behalf right now. At this very moment He is praying for us. When we suffer, He understands. In our trials we are blessed by the comfort of our Savior. This great fact is a source of comfort for Elsie and me.

Second, there is the comfort of the Spirit. Before our Lord died on the cross, He said to His disciples, "And I will pray the Father, and he shall give you another Comforter, that he may abide with you for ever; even the Spirit of truth. . . . I will not leave you comfortless" (John 14:16-18). Here we have our Lord's promise that after His departure He would send the Holy Spirit to carry on the ministry of comfort.

It is recorded of the churches in Judea, Galilee, and Samaria that they "were edified; and walking in the fear of the Lord, and in the comfort of the Holy Ghost, were multiplied" (Acts 9:31). This is written testimony of the fulfillment of Christ's promise that another Comforter would come to minister to His church. Those suffering and persecuted Christians were strengthened by "the comfort of the Holy Spirit."

Like the Savior's comfort, the Spirit's comfort is for believers. It is only for those who have received the Lord Jesus Christ as Savior. You see, when a sinner trusts

Christ, the Holy Spirit enters his body to take up perma-
nent residence. All truly saved persons, without exception,
are indwelt by the Holy Spirit (Romans 8:9; 1 Corinthians
3:16; 6:19-20). This is a pertinent and precious truth,
particularly when one is experiencing suffering or sorrow.

When J. Sidlow Baxter's wife died, he was living in
California. I was in Florida at that time, so I telephoned
him to express my sympathy and to offer any assistance
that might be needed. When he answered my call, it was
obvious he was in deep sorrow. But I shall never forget
what he said: "Lehman, I am very lonely, but I am not
alone. I am being comforted." I knew what he meant. He
had walked daily in fellowship with the Holy Spirit, so in
his sorrow he experienced the Spirit's comfort.

A woman had taken a trip to the Holy Land and was
relating her experience. She said, "Never in my life have I
felt so near to God. I plan to make the trip again. It will
be worth the money I spend to be so near to God again."

Well, thank God I need not wait for a trip to Israel to
experience God's nearness. These are days when Elsie and
I need comfort. Right now I am painfully conscious of my
own weakness and inadequacy. But I am also aware of the
Holy Spirit's presence in me, along with His bountiful
provision. As I write, we are being comforted. One of
Paul's prayers for the Christians at Ephesus is being answered now in our behalf: "That He would grant you,
according to the riches of his glory, to be strengthened
with might by his Spirit in the inner man" (Ephesians
3:16).

I am not suggesting that the way is easy. In my best
moments I am aware of dangerous and devilish intrusions
into my mind. The Christian life is a conflict. "For the
flesh lusteth against the Spirit, and the Spirit against the
flesh: and these are contrary the one to the other: so that
ye cannot do the things that ye would" (Galatians 5:17). If
we give way to the sinful nature in us, we grieve the Holy
Spirit and miss His comfort. But when we are controlled

by Him, He is a strong Comforter in our infirmities and afflictions.

Third, there is the comfort of the Scriptures. The apostle Paul wrote, "For whatsoever things were written aforetime were written for our learning, that we through patience and *comfort of the scriptures* might have hope" (Romans 15:4). How much do we really know in our personal experience about the comfort of the Scriptures?

Quite honestly, until our recent trial, I had never been put to the test in my own personal life. I saw how God's Word comforted others in their trials and sorrows as I read it to sick, suffering, and bereaved Christians. I could vouch for the truth and accuracy of Hebrews 4:12, which says, "For the word of God is quick, and powerful, and sharper than any twoedged sword, piercing even to the dividing asunder of soul and spirit, and of the joints and marrow, and is a discerner of the thoughts and intents of the heart." I knew that Word had quickened and saved me in 1927, and I had witnessed its power to comfort others.

But now I am the person passing through the fiery trial. Now I am in need of comfort. I recalled the times I expounded Hebrews 4:12, emphasizing the importance of the word "quick" or "alive." I explained that the Greek verb *azo*, a present participle, means that God's Word is continuously alive and active. The Bible is not a dead letter; it is not passive nor passe. It is continuously at work, producing and preserving spiritual life.

Then too, the Word of God is powerful. The Greek word translated "powerful" is *energes*, from which we get our English word *energy*. It is powerful enough to reach the innermost recesses of each of us, down deep where we really hurt. Paul could have had all this in mind when he spoke of "the comfort of the scriptures."

One reason the Scriptures were written was to comfort God's children in times of sickness, suffering, and sorrow. The learning we glean from the Bible is for the everyday experiences of life, and comfort is one of the needs the Scriptures supply. The very fact that Paul quoted from the Old Testament tells us that he depended upon the Scriptures for consolation and encouragement. Comfort is one of the blessings God gives to us through His Word.

An important factor is that we must receive the Word of God in faith. God's truth must be appropriated with implicit trust, and with no mental reservations whatsoever. Paul expressed this idea clearly in his first epistle to the Thessalonians when he wrote, "For this cause also thank we God without ceasing, because, when ye received the word of God which ye heard of us, ye received it not as the word of men, but as it is in truth, the word of God, which effectually worketh also in you that believe" (1 Thessalonians 2:13). The mere reading of some portion of Scripture or listening to someone expound it is not sufficient in itself. The Word must be applied. James said, "But be ye doers of the word and not hearers only, deceiving your own selves" (James 1:22).

The Bible has been our guidebook throughout the years of our marriage. We believed it, taught it to our children, and sought to obey its precepts. We knew it worked. But now we are facing a severe personal trial. It has afforded us an excellent opportunity to prove the Bible's effectiveness in the hour of affliction and adversity. Elsie was helpless, unable to read. So it was left to me to find comfort in the Scriptures and then to share it with her. In my heart has come a deeper hunger for God's Word. In fact, my desire to listen to God speak to me is greater than my desire to pray. When I pray, I speak to God. When I read God's Word, He speaks to me, and I need to know what He has to say in the dark hour.

While Elsie was in the hospital, each morning I would thank Him for blessings and mercies, which I mentioned one by one. Then, after a request for guidance, I would go immediately to the Word. After I read and meditated quietly, I selected a verse, typed it on a 3 by 5 card, and began my drive to the hospital. On the way down I memorized the verse. Throughout the day I read it to Elsie at intervals, and before leaving her at night we would recite it together. This became our daily practice, and it continues to be the main source of strength and comfort to us.

Here are a few of the verses God used to sustain and comfort us: Deuteronomy 33:27; Joshua 1:8; Psalm 23; 27:1; 34:19; 37:1-7, 25; 42:5, 11; 46:1; 48:14; 55:22; 84:11; 103:10-14; 119:50, 75; Isaiah 26:3; 41:10; Lamentations 3:22-23, 32; Romans 8:28-32; 1 Corinthians 10:13; 2 Corinthians 1:3-4; Ephesians 3:16; Philippians 4:4, 6, 7; Colossians 3:16; 1 Thessalonians 4:16-17; 5:18; Hebrews 12:6; 1 Peter 5:7.

As I write these lines, it is almost two years since our trial began. The Word of God is our stronghold. God remains faithful, and His grace continues to be sufficient. We are confident that He who began His good work in us will carry it on to completion, until our Lord Jesus Christ returns (Philippians 1:6). In that day "we shall be like him; for we shall see him as he is" (1 John 3:2).

God has various ways of getting our attention in order to show how much He loves us. His dealings with us are based on perfect principles. It may surprise you to discover what wonderful things God will do for us and through us when we allow Him to work unhindered in our lives. His principle of discipline is never pleasant, but it leads to purity and peace.

9

That Strange Love of God

Many Christians, including preachers, songwriters, poets, and others, have as their favorite subject "the love of God." I doubt if some of them know the meaning of the word *love*. They use it as sort of a cover-all for ills—physical, spiritual, and moral. Tell people that God loves them and they feel good. They go away cheerful and lighthearted. One preacher closes his service with the following benediction: "God loves you, and so do I." Now there is nothing wrong with that statement, nor would I question the preacher's sincerity and honesty when he tells the people he loves them. But when the Christian is really hurting, it is difficult to reconcile the love of God with human affliction and suffering. Recently a Christian lady said to me, "If God loves me, why does He make me suffer?" Her problem lay with her lack of understanding of God's love.

The Bible tells us it is a *strange* love. "Behold, what manner of love the Father hath bestowed upon us, that we should be called the sons of God" (1 John 3:1). Note that word *manner*. The Greek word is *potapos*, an adjective

that describes something strange or foreign—as from another country. It does not merely convey the idea of greatness as some modern translations have it. When our Lord
rebuked the winds and calmed the stormy sea, "The men
marvelled, saying, What *manner* of man is this, that even
the winds and the sea obey him!" (Matthew 8:27, italics
added). They saw something they had never witnessed
before. When they saw the miracle, they thought, *This
man is out of this world. What we saw is strange and
foreign.*

We see that "out of this world" love in action in Romans 5:8: "But God commendeth his love toward us, in
that, while we were yet sinners, Christ died for us." It is a
strange love that would cause a father to put his only son
to death for the sins of wicked people, especially when the
Son Himself is righteous and holy. We know nothing of
that kind of love. It is foreign to us because it came from
another world. It was never a part of human civilization.
Never had any person on earth witnessed that kind of
love. "Herein is love, not that we loved God, but that He
loved us, and sent his Son to be the propitiation for our
sins" (1 John 4:10). That foreign kind of love boggles our
minds. Whether or not we can understand it, the amazing
fact remains that it is blessedly real—God sent His sinless
Son to die for us sinners. *What manner of love!*

That brings us to consider seriously this strange love
of God at work in the lives of His children. It is explained
in one of those passages we prefer to pass by. "For whom
the Lord loveth he chasteneth, and scourgeth every son
whom he receiveth" (Hebrews 12:6).

Dear reader, if you are a true child of God, and by
true child of God I mean that you have had a genuine
born-again experience, then here is a truth you must discover experientially. You and I must learn—and never
drift away from—the truth that the strange love of God
prompts Him to chasten us. Let us consider this verse in
its context.

Consider the Exhortation

The very thought of a God of love chastening His children is not acceptable to most of us. As children growing up we all had the idea in our minds that our parents showed love to us when they gave us those things we wanted and enjoyed. But when they placed restrictions upon us we jumped hastily to the conclusion that they didn't love us. We could understand love that coddled and comforted us, but we could not reconcile love with chastening and correction.

The Christians to whom the epistle of Hebrews was first addressed were Jews. They were a minority group who believed Jesus Christ was their promised Messiah. Their unbelieving Jewish brothers had ostracized them. Unbelieving Gentiles despised them. They could not find employment. The persecution was difficult for them to bear. If they had made the right move by embracing Christianity, why did they suffer those things? If God loved them, should He not deliver them from suffering and persecution? They had been taught that God loved all sinners and that He sent His Son to die for them. They believed the message, but now all they knew was adversity and affliction. Was that the way God showed love to His children? Obviously there was something about the love of God they had not learned.

The Holy Spirit directed His penman to write words that would meet the need of their hearts. He begins by drawing their attention to a portion of their own Old Testament Scriptures that had been forgotten, saying, *"Ye have forgotten the exhortation which speaketh unto you as unto children"* (Hebrews 12:5). He brings them back to the written Word of God, the one source of truth for every child of God. He quotes the voice of God speaking directly to them. Notice he says, *"Ye* have forgotten the exhortation which speaketh unto *you"* (italics added). Some expositors have rendered this statement interrogatively to read, "Have ye forgotten the exhortation?" And what was the important truth they carelessly let slip from them? It was that strange aspect of God's love: "My son, despise not thou the chastening of the Lord, nor faint when thou art rebuked of him: For whom the Lord loveth He chasteneth, and scourgeth every son whom He receiveth" (Hebrews 12:5-6).

Forgetfulness can be a deadly thing. How foolish we are when we forget God's words. And take notice which of His words we are inclined to forget, namely, words of *exhortation*. The word *exhort* (Greek: *parakaleo*) means to admonish or to urge the pursuit of some course of conduct. It was the word of exhortation those Jewish believers forgot, not the words of God's unconditional convenant, not God's promise of everlasting life. The Scripture to which the writer pointed them is Proverbs 3:11-12: "My son, despise not the chastening of the Lord; neither be weary of his correction: For whom the Lord loveth he correcteth; even as a father the son in whom he delighteth.

Bible study can be attractive and interesting, and even exciting to some Christians as long as it does not make demands on them. They can enjoy long discourses on the love of God as long as the teaching does not cut into their life-style. They may never forget God's words in Jeremiah 31:3: "I have loved thee with an everlasting love" or in John 3:16 where our Lord said, "For God so loved the world, that he gave his only begotten Son, that whosoever believeth in him should not perish, but have everlasting life." Why remember certain verses that speak of God's love, and forget others? It is because we pick and choose. We wilfully forget that strange, foreign chastening love of God.

Sit down sometime and read through the book of Deuteronomy. There you will hear God saying repeatedly, "Remember . . . and forget not." Mark each appearance of the words *remember* and *forget*. The two hours you will spend in this spiritual exercise will be most rewarding.

Consider the Explanation

In chapter 11 of Hebrews the writer points out the fact that many Old Testament believers have suffered. He takes his illustration from several periods of biblical history and shows how men and women from various walks of life suffered adversity and affliction. They faced incredible odds for the glory of God. And the God of Old Testament history is the same God Christians worship today.

In chapter 12 the Christian is shown how to view the trials and tribulations of life. The key word in verses 5-11 is *chastening,* appearing in different forms not less than seven times. The Greek word is *paideia,* which comes from *pais,* meaning "child." It is a term used broadly for the means parents use to train their children. God too has methods for chastening His children, and whatever method He uses is sent for our good. A life without discipline can have no value.

The chastening of the Lord conveys His love. "For whom the Lord loveth He chasteneth, and scourgeth every son whom He receiveth (Hebrews 12:6). It would not be an indication of a father's love to allow a child to do whatever he pleases. The discipline of God is always motivated by love. It confirms, or proves, God's love for us. There is a tender, parental love behind the disciplines of our heavenly Father. God is not acting here as a judge, but as a father with our well-being in view. Even the most dreadful disappointments, the most terrible trials are appointed by perfect wisdom and sent by pure love. We may think this a strange way to convey love, but then we must keep in mind the fact that the love of God is a *strange* love, foreign and alien to fallen man. Regardless of how we may feel, chastisement does convey the love of God.

The chastening of the Lord confirms our sonship. "If ye endure chastening, God dealeth with you as with sons; for what son is he whom the father chasteneth not? But if ye be without chastisement, whereof all her partakers, then are ye bastards, and not sons" (Hebrews 12:7-8). Hebrews

is addressed to children of God, so chastening is actually a
mark of sonship. No doubt there were those among the
believing Hebrews who were merely professing to have
faith and who had not been born again. They would never
understand a God who does with His children as He pleases
rather than pleasing them. What God wants for us is
higher and nobler than what any thoughtful earthly parent wants for his child.

There is no way that one can conceive of sonship
without chastisement. Those who are without chastisement and claim to be sons of God are making a false
claim. The greatest saints of the past suffered adversity
and affliction. They knew they possessed everlasting life
because they believed in the Lord Jesus Christ as their
personal Savior (John 3:16; 5:24); because they experienced God leading them (Romans 8:14); because God's
Spirit witnessed to their spirits (Romans 8:15-16); and
because they experienced the discipline of God in their
lives. If professing Christians are without chastening, they
are illegitimate, not true sons. So declares the Word of
God.

The chastening of the Lord corrects our faults. "Furthermore we have had fathers of our flesh which corrected
us, and we gave them reverence: shall we not much rather
be in subjection unto the Father of spirits, and live?"
(Hebrews 12:9). Our earthly father is called a "corrector"
(Greek: *paidentēs*), meaning a "chastiser." To correct is to
restore to a right state. Wrongs must be made right, and
the crooked must be made straight. Every Christian has
faults and failures that require correcting (James 3:2).
Our earthly parents corrected us and rightly so because of
our relationship to them. If it was proper for us to submit
to their corrections, how much more should we submit to
our heavenly Father! When we were born again we received a new nature, the very nature of God, so that we
are said to be "partakers of the divine nature" (2 Peter
1:4). However, in every Christian the possibility of sinning
in thought, word, and deed remains. The sins we commit

as Christians must be confessed and forsaken: "For if we would judge ourselves, we should not be judged. But when we are judged, we are chastened of the Lord, that we should not be condemned with the world" (1 Corinthians 11:31-32). Paul is saying that if Christians would use discernment, that is, if we would distinguish between what we are and what God requires us to be, we would not need to be chastened of the Lord. If we really knew ourselves as we actually are and judged ourselves accordingly, we would not need the Lord's chastening. The Corinthians were being chastened, not because they were unbelievers, but because they were Christ's own. Beloved, let us test ourselves daily and arrive at a true estimate of ourselves (1 Corinthians 11:28). Let us never rest until every known sin is confessed and forsaken.

The chastening of the Lord curbs our temperaments. We do not all have the same dispositions. Personality traits differ. If we will not control our weaknesses, God will use His fatherly method of chastisement. A proverb says, "He that covereth his sins shall not prosper: but whoso confesseth and forsaketh them shall have mercy" (Proverbs 28:13). Sometimes God's chastenings, rather than being corrective, are preventive. When God chastens He does not act capriciously but with care and consideration for our well-being and welfare. Again, let us be reminded that the chastening of the Lord is ministered in tender love. And it is His sovereign right to discipline us whenever and however He chooses.

The apostle Paul had a tendency toward pride. It was a sin that had not been eradicated from his life and needed to be curbed. He wrote about it in his second epistle to the Corinthians: "And lest I should be exalted above measure through the abundance of the revelations, there was given to me a thorn in the flesh, the messenger of Satan to buffet me, lest I should be exalted above measure" (2 Corinthians 12:7). Notice that this verse commences and concludes with the exact same phrase, "lest I should be exalted above measure." We might assume from this that

Paul was inclined toward a haughty exaltation of self, the common sin of "being lifted up with pride" (1 Timothy 3:6) or being "highminded" (1 Timothy 6:17). Through the chastening love of God, Paul learned the lesson so well that he could write, "For I say, through the grace given unto me, to every man that is among you, not to think of himself more highly than he ought to think; but to think soberly, according as God hath dealt to every man the measure of faith" (Romans 12:3).

When we discover a weakness within ourselves, we should act at once to curb it. If we neglect it and allow it to grow, the Lord will step in and chasten us in order to prevent further damage to us and our testimony for Him. Yet we ourselves can prevent His chastening by dealing with that particular sin. An ounce of prevention is worth more than a ton of cure. Chastening is one of God's blessings. Do we thank Him for it?

The chastening of the Lord cleanses our sins. "Furthermore we have had fathers of our flesh which corrected us, and we gave them reverence: shall we not much rather be in subjection unto the Father of spirits, and live? For they verily for a few days chastened us after their own pleasure; but he for our profit, that we might be partakers of his holiness" (Hebrews 12:9-10). The word translated "holiness" is *hagiasmos*, which means "sanctification." The idea conveyed here is separation unto God. It is not merely a positional sanctification, but it includes practical sanctification, a behavior befitting those who are separated. Paul used the same word when he wrote, "For God hath not called us unto uncleanness, but unto holiness" (1 Thessalonians 4:7) and "But now being made free from sin, and become servants to God, ye have your fruit unto holiness, and the end everlasting life" (Romans 6:22).

The fruit of holiness should be the course of life befitting all sons of God. Positionally we enter into that separation unto God by faith in Jesus Christ. The Holy Spirit sanctifies (sets apart) every believer at the time of his salvation (1 Corinthians 6:11), the ground of positional sanctification being the death of Christ (Hebrews 10:10, 29; 13:12). However, God's purpose in saving us through the death of His Son is that we should be separated from evil thoughts, words, and deeds: "For this is the will of God, even your sanctification, that ye should abstain from fornication" (1 Thessalonians 4:3). We all should pursue holiness earnestly and diligently. We learn it as we read, study, and obey the Word of God (Psalm 119:9, 11; John 15:3; 17:17, 19; 1 Peter 2:2).

If, on the other hand, we neglect the pursuit of holiness, then God steps in to chasten us. "As many as I love, I rebuke and chasten: be zealous therefore, and repent" (Revelation 3:19). And when He does, we must accept the discipline as coming from Him, not to harm us but to point us toward our highest and ultimate good. The chastening from God is designed to make us wiser and better Christians. I sincerely doubt the possibility of any Christian becoming spiritually mature and continuing in fellowship with God except through God's chastening.

Consider the Expectation

The verses in the passage we are considering suggest three ways in which we can react to God's discipline.

We can despise it. "My son, despise not thou the chastening of the Lord" (Hebrews 12:5). The word *despise* (*exoutheneō*) means "to make light of, to treat with contempt." We should never consider the chastening of the Lord as a thing of no account or no value. Anything that is "for our profit" (Hebrews 12:10) is a thing not to be despised. When I was a pastor in Detroit, a twenty-one-year-old young man was killed riding his motorcycle on the John Lodge Expressway. Though his mother was a professing Christian, she became bitter and angry with God. She would not accept the trial as from the Lord. I tried to explain to her that she was not expected to take her problem lightly, but neither was she to take the Lord's chastening through the problem lightly. God is in control, and He always has a good and wise purpose in chastening His children. Christians do suffer. "Many are the afflictions of the righteous" (Psalm 34:19). "Man is born unto trouble, as the sparks fly upward" (Job 5:7). "In the world ye shall have tribulation" (John 16:33). "Yea, and all that will live godly in Christ Jesus shall suffer persecution" (2 Timothy 3:12). We expect disciplines in this life, but we must never despise them.

We can faint under it. "Nor faint when thou art rebuked of him" (Hebrews 12:5). The Greek word is *ekluō* and it means to grow weary, to lose heart. The Christian is a pilgrim, a sojourner who is ever on the move. He is going somewhere. The goal is conformity to the likeness of our Lord Jesus Christ who endured the cross and despised the shame. Christ Himself is our example—He never lost heart. "Consider him that endured such contradiction of sinners against himself, lest ye be wearied and faint in your minds" (Hebrews 12:3). This is a good verse to read when the trials of life cause us to grow weary. We are told to pause and give serious thought to the sufferings of Christ. Learn with perception what He endured when He was here on earth. When we are spending time daily in the Word of God, the Holy Spirit can take the things of Christ and reveal them plainly to us. This enables us to persevere with patience. "And let us not be weary in well doing: for in due season we shall reap, if we faint not" (Galatians 6:9).

We can accept it as coming from a loving Father. "Now no chastening for the present seemeth to be joyous, but grievous: nevertheless afterward it yieldeth the peaceable fruit of righteousness unto them which are exercised thereby" (Hebrews 12:11). The disciplines of the Lord are never without plan or purpose. They are never an afterthought on His part. When God chastens us He is seeking to accomplish something in us for our good and His glory. So that with every chastening act of God there is a bright expectation, something good to which we can look forward. The writer calls it God's "afterward." And we may be certain that our Father's discipline will never bring disappointment. Don't neglect God's afterwards and hereafters. Some of them contain promises that light up our future with hope and expectancy.

"Nevertheless *afterward* it yieldeth the peaceable fruit of righteousness unto them which are exercised thereby." (Hebrews 12:11, italics added)

"What I do thou knowest not now; but thou shalt know *hereafter*." (John 13:7, italics added)

"Thou shalt guide me with thy counsel, and *afterward* receive me to glory." (Psalm 73:24, italics added)

In conclusion, take special notice of the fact that the blessings of chastisement come to them "which are exercised thereby." We are to be *exercised* by our trials and tribulations. The Greek word is *gumnazō*, which means to train the body or the mind with a view to holiness and righteousness. As we accept chastening and are trained by it, we learn that it is one of God's richest blessings.

We are finding that physical therapy for my wife in her paralyzed condition is difficult and painful. It is never convenient or comfortable to go through treatments, but she endures them with the hope and expectation of improvement.

How much more should we exercise ourselves to be trained by our heavenly Father's chastening. The writer of Hebrews makes this point in chapter 5. He speaks of the failure of believers to study the deeper truths of God's Word. All such remain spiritual infants and thus continue inexperienced and unskillful in handling life's problems: "But strong meat belongeth to them that are of full age, even those who by reason of use have their senses exercised to discern both good and evil" (Hebrews 5:14).

Growing spiritually is not merely a matter of time. It

is not an experience that comes with the years as does physical growth. A young man invited me to his home for dinner. He said he wanted me to meet his wife and a daughter who was six years old. If the little girl was six and her mother was thirty years old, I had a good idea of what to expect when I saw them just by knowing their ages.

But that is not true in the realm of spiritual experience. It is possible that a person who has been saved six years could be further advanced spiritually than one saved for thirty years. In spiritual matters some Christians are "dull of hearing" (Hebrews 5:11). They have ceased to be eager hearers and doers of the Word. Thus they are no longer exercised by it and no longer grow spiritually. The adjective used in this verse is the Greek word *nothroi* and suggests sluggishness or laziness. It is a condition one acquires when he loses his eagerness for the Word of God.

Some Christians are exercised by their trials while others are not. Some resent chastening and resent God while others accept God's discipline and advance because of it. The Bible does not require believers to enjoy chastening, but we are expected to regard it rightly and react to it properly. When we come to grips with God's reason for chastening us, it will lead to a profitable afterward. Suffering must be borne in the right spirit if we are to profit from it. "For I reckon that the sufferings of this present time are not worthy to be compared with the glory which shall be revealed in us" (Romans 8:18).

Conclusion

Our trial is not over. But as I conclude this book, let me share with you the precious lesson Elsie and I have learned as God has been comforting us. Look again with me at 2 Corinthians 1:4: "Who comforteth us in all our tribulation, that we may be able to comfort them which are in any trouble, by the comfort wherewith we ourselves are comforted of God." The comfort of God in our trial has been a part of His training program for us. He has been preparing us so that we can minister to others.

Since Elsie's stroke on March 27, 1982, the number of persons on our prayer list has multiplied more than six times. We have a feeling of empathy and sympathy for others, such as we had not experienced before. It was given to us by God so that we might pass it on to the suffering and sorrowing people whose lives we touch.

Letters and telephone calls from many parts of our nation and Canada have come to us requesting prayer. So many people are hurting in this world! Through our time in God's waiting room, a new dimension has been added to our ministry—bringing comfort to others. This is at once a privilege and a responsibility. And we have learned that as we offer comfort to others, we ourselves are comforted.

Moody Press, a ministry of the Moody Bible Institute, is designed for education, evangelization, and edification. If we may assist you in knowing more about Christ and the Christian life, please write us without obligation: Moody Press, % MLM, Chicago, Illinois 60610.